Too Early Frost

Also by Gerald Oosterveen:

Serving Mentally Impaired People: A Resource Guide for Pastors and Church Workers
(With Bruce L. Cook)

Too Early Frost

by Gerald Oosterveen

A Father's Account
of the
Death of His Son

Zondervan Books
Zondervan Publishing House
Grand Rapids, Michigan

TOO EARLY FROST: A FATHER'S ACCOUNT OF THE DEATH OF HIS SON
Copyright © 1988 by Gerald Oosterveen

Zondervan Books
are published by Zondervan Publishing House
1415 Lake Drive, S.E.
Grand Rapids, MI 49506

Library of Congress Cataloging in Publication Data

Oosterveen, Gerald.
    Too early frost : a father's account of the death of his son / Gerald
Oosterveen.
        p. cm.
    ISBN 0-310-37771-4
    1. Children—Death—Religious aspects—Christianity. 2. Tumors in
children—Religious aspects—Christianity. 3. Bereavement—Religious aspects—Christianity. 4. Oosterveen, Gerald. 5. Oosterveen, Gerard
Richard, 1961–1970. 6. Fathers and sons. 7. Consolation. I. Title.
BV4907.067   1988
248.8'6'0924—dc19   8735301
                                                               CIP

Unless otherwise noted, all Scripture references are taken from the Holy
Bible: New International Version (North American Edition), copyright
© 1973, 1978, 1984 by the International Bible Society. Used by
permission of Zondervan Bible Publishers.

Printed in the United States of America

88 89 90 91 92 93 / CH / 10 9 8 7 6 5 4 3 2

To Ruth,
the boy's mother,
who also lived this story

But he knows the way that I take;
when he has tested me,
I will come forth as gold.
—Job 23:10

Contents

prologue ❦

A special bond exists between a man and his first child. The child, in a sense, confirms the man's manhood, the fact that he is capable of fathering a child. Though being able to beget children is no longer a test of manhood as it was in previous ages, it still counts for something—even in our culture of confused feelings about the value of children. Overnight, the birth of this first child changed the man into a father.

Expertise, though, is another matter. That is learned with the passing of time. Precisely because the father learns about the joys, frustrations, and mistakes of fathering through the relationship with this first child, the bond ordinarily becomes stronger than those between him and other children in the family. And it remains special.

The current emphasis on the equality of the sexes notwithstanding, it is usually a matter of special pride when the first child is a son. The son will carry on the father's family name, unlike a daughter who will likely change her name when she marries and whose children will bear a different name. This perpetuation of the name continues the stream of the generations. It gives to the father a sense of immortality. Something will survive him. A son, too, makes a father dream of the day when they can go hunting together or fishing—though there is no good

11

reason why fathers and daughters or mothers and sons cannot do the same thing. There's still something special about this whole idea of being a man, however, and of having a son who will become a man like his father, except that possibly he will achieve all those dreams the father never quite realized.

The birth of my firstborn was a matter of great pride for me, especially because he was a son. I don't deny it, even now. He was special in a way that a firstborn daughter probably never would have been. That may be because I never knew my father, never experienced that beautiful father-son relationship until I had already lived a quarter-century.

Perhaps that is why, when my firstborn son became ill, the long drawn-out period during which he suffered was so intensely painful for me. In a real sense, part of me suffered with him and, in the end, died with him, something that will never be recaptured regardless of how much time may pass. Because of the impairment of my second son and because my third child is a daughter, both infinitely precious but unable to carry on our family name, this first son was the link between past and future generations, a link that was snapped so unexpectedly and with such absolute finality.

The story that follows is our story, my son's and mine. Purposely, I don't use my son's name because, in a sense, I want this to be a universal story. The boy was *my* son, but he could have been anyone's son—perhaps your son, who lived in your home. But I can only write about what happened to us. I make no apology for that, nor explain why I share so little about the feelings of the others involved, including the boy's mother, and the part played by them. I simply describe what it was like for this boy who became so ill and me, and how we related to each other, and how we coped with this unequal struggle against cancer. If the narrow scope of this story appears selfish, forgive me. But please read on, beyond the poem I wrote recently, to the very end of the book and then judge, if you must.

Shards

The jagged shards
of yesterday
tucked away
in the
rag bag of my memories
are sharp
today as ever.
And every time
I rummage there
I bleed again
though
there are soft things
too.

Too Early Frost

one ⧢

A thin layer of freshly fallen leaves, glued to the sidewalk by the early morning dew, crunched under our feet as we hurried the few blocks to the hospital from the guest house where we were staying. We pulled our coats snugly around us as protection against a chilly breeze that blew from the opposite direction. It was still quite dark, despite the full October moon that hung low in the western sky. The moon wore a halo, a bright, complete circle so well defined that in a few places there was a hint of color, almost like a rainbow.

"That circle's called a *corona*," I explained to my wife as we walked. "Neighbor Jas calls it a *moondog*. He says it signals a change in the weather; the brighter the circle, the more drastic the change will be. The halo's really the diffraction of the moonbeams through tiny droplets of moisture that have crystallized around specks of dust suspended in the upper atmosphere."

She was not really interested in atmospheric phenomena just then, nor was I. It was a matter of making small talk, aimless chatter to get our minds off the frightening prospect we faced this morning. On another day we would have lingered to drink in deeply the serenity of such a fine autumn dawn as this, but not today. The grandeur of God's heavens could not overcome the sense of foreboding that chilled our hearts far more than the wind could ever chill our bodies.

When we reached the hospital well before six, the security guard only glanced at the special pass that told him we were to be admitted this early because of a scheduled surgery. He had seen so many of them that they held no special meaning anymore; for us it was an alarming first. Another couple boarded the elevator that swiftly lifted us to Pediatrics. Briefly I wondered whether they also had a child in surgery this morning, then concluded there could not possibly be any other reason for them to be here at this time. Like us, they hid behind a wall of apprehensive silence.

Our son was already awake and welcomed us happily when we walked into his room. As though waiting for our arrival, a nurse came to give the boy an injection to help him drift off into the anesthetic sleep that would shield him from the pain of surgery. As he turned over, I glimpsed the bulge just left of his lower spine that was the reason for our being here and the cause of our deep concern. The bulge hid a tumor, doctors had said four days earlier, but without surgery there was no way of telling whether it was benign or malignant. Today, in just a few hours, we would know. We were torn between desperately wanting to know the truth and being afraid to hear it.

The boy did not know the uncertainty that faced him. All he knew was that today's surgery might end the pain that had so long troubled him. He welcomed that prospect, yet despite the bravery with which he had faced this second hospital stay of his short life, surgery was something else. The surgeon, a kind, grandfatherly man who had a way with children, had stopped by the previous evening to explain in simple terms just what would happen. He had been honest and direct, telling the boy that, though the next few days he would have much pain, it should remove the other pain he always felt. We had added our reassuring words to his, but the boy, only partially convinced, had gone to sleep soon after.

How does one prepare a little boy who has just turned six for the discomfort and pain of surgery without stirring up in him an overpowering apprehension that might interfere with the healing process? This morning the boy wanted to hear us say again that we would stay with him until he fell asleep and be there still when he awoke after surgery. We promised. Nothing could have enticed us to be anywhere else, even while we wished we were a thousand miles away.

Before long he became drowsy. An orderly came to help the nurse lift him onto the gurney. The nurse said that there was no point in our staying in the hospital for the next several hours, so she suggested we get breakfast. We walked beside the boy down the hall and into the elevator. When he was wheeled out onto the surgical floor, we watched the doors close behind him, those green barricades marked "No Admittance" that seemed to say that parents were now unnecessary. A feeling of helplessness surged over me; there was nothing I could do for him now. How I wished I could go with him, hold his hand, make everything all right again. But it was out of my hands and in the hands of the surgeons. That both the boy and his tumor were also in the hands of God did not occur to me. Had someone mentioned it, the words would have brought little comfort.

Whatever we may have talked about at breakfast has escaped me. During the frequent periods of silence I thought back over the previous seven years. They had not been easy. We were married after my first year in college, facing three more years of college followed by three years of seminary. Though I worked part-time during those student years, and my wife worked full-time for the first few, money was never plentiful. Somehow we made ends meet, taking out student loans and sacrificing things others took for granted, yet doing so willingly because we were working toward a worthwhile goal. Our marriage had rocky stretches as we attempted to grow together. It is not easy for two people with such different temperaments and from divergent backgrounds to become one. But we tried and we had hope.

My wife became pregnant in the second year of our marriage. We had not planned it that way, but it happened nonetheless. I was apprehensive about expenses and fearful of the responsibilities of parenthood. Being a husband was difficult enough, and I was not always doing well at that.

When the boy was born, however, another feeling seemed to override my fears: the pride of fatherhood. Here was another generation, the first in the new world to bear our family name. We named him after my father who had died young in the old world just before I was born. My name is a variation on my father's name too. I was the link between the old and the new, between death and life.

It all seemed so long ago. In my mind I could still see the beautiful blond-haired baby with the sparkling blue eyes—healthy, quick, and intelligent. He quickly captured our hearts and our world changed drastically to accommodate his presence. Like parents of any first-born, we experienced our on-the-job training as an exciting, yet frightening time. He, in turn, soaked up our love and returned it with interest. God was so good in giving us such a fine little boy. When we took him for rides in his stroller, he smiled at people as they came over to talk to him. Curious about everything, he was full of questions, always eager to see how something worked. He developed his own unique language. "Pooby noony" was his name for the paper boy. Applesauce became "lalak" in his book. It was a good time, and we were for the most part content.

One day he plugged in the iron and then went on to something else. We only noticed it after a pointed dark spot was burned into the carpet. Another time, as he played in the backyard, he wound a piece of rope tightly around his neck but realized the danger before it was too late; it had begun to hurt, he said. Then there was the time he ate most of a bottle of chewable vitamins, and the time he drank a bottle of ink. The poison control center told my wife to induce vomiting. By what law is it governed that little boys only vomit when they are not supposed to, and preferably in any convenient place except the bathroom, but have cast-iron stomachs when one tries to make them vomit?

There was the morning we found him in the flour-coated kitchen because he had decided to surprise mom by baking a pie. And the morning, when he was still only three, that he decided to go for an early morning walk in his pajamas. We awoke when we heard a child's cries outside and were galvanized into action when we realized they sounded familiar. A dog had frightened him a block away, and he had decided there was, after all, no place like home.

Then there was that last summer of my seminary years when we served a small country church. With his toy bulldozer he created endlessly winding roads across the gravel driveway. That completed, he got his little cars and zipped through the twists and turns, racing against himself for best time. He loved trips to the zoo and hikes in the forest. His boundless energy kept us on our toes and, when channeled into game activities, it kept him busy. He loved to play harmless pranks on me, and I remembered with pangs of regret how one time when I was in a foul mood I spanked him for it when he had really done no wrong.

When a little brother appeared on the scene just after

his third birthday, the boy was thrilled. Unaware that his brother was developing more slowly than normal, he would hang over the crib railing to play peekaboo until the baby laughed. That difficult year, as we gradually came to realize that our second son had suffered neurological damage before or during birth and would be retarded, we appreciated all the more the vivacity of our first one. The anguish of having a disabled child was diminished somewhat by having another who was, by all indications, normal.

Was that, I wondered, why this beautiful first son, the one of whom we were so proud, became ill? Was it God's way of teaching us an important lesson about the value of individuals? Had he decided to take from us a healthy son because we received less than enthusiastically the one who was impaired? But by that time we loved both equally! Or did God allow our older son to become ill to test our love, my love, like he tested the love and faith of Abraham so long ago on Mount Moriah? I wondered, but I didn't know.

I graduated from seminary when the boy was almost five. It was an exciting time. I was eager to begin serving a church. A few months later we moved to a small town where I was ordained and installed in the ministry. Though our son reluctantly left his city friends behind, he made new friends quickly. But there was a difference now. He was now a minister's son.

The first indication that he was not well came within six months after the move. Always a picture of health, never before sick, he began to complain occasionally about pain in his left thigh. Some nights he cried in his sleep. Looking over some pictures we had recently taken, we noticed that his favorite posture was to stand bent over with his hands on his knees or with his left leg perched on a rock or other slightly elevated object.

Visits to the doctor were frustrating and fruitless. By the

time he reached the doctor's office, the pain was always gone and the boy would skip around the office in high spirits. After several visits, the doctor shook his head a little impatiently and remarked that there was nothing to worry about.

"The boy's got growing pains. Don't take it so seriously. He'll outgrow them."

When the pain persisted and my wife kept bringing the boy back, the doctor, who was by this time just as frustrated as we were, said to her, "There still is nothing wrong with the boy. Perhaps it would be good for you to see a psychologist. You're imagining things and planting silly ideas in the boy's head."

I was not much help. Though I had observed the boy's response to his pain, I told my wife that the doctor undoubtedly knew what he was talking about and we should just ignore the crying. It was cowardice, I now realize, putting my head into the sand while hoping that this troublesome pain would simply vanish and bother us no more. Consequently, this was not a happy time for any of us.

One day when he once again came into the house crying with pain, I abandoned my ostrich policy and offered the boy a dollar if he would please tell the doctor this time where it hurt. The bribe did not work because again the pain was gone by the time we reached the doctor's office. On a camping vacation that summer, the pain became more intense, aggravated perhaps by the cool nights in our tent camper. He was hospitalized, but a week of testing revealed no hint as to the source of the trouble. Yet the pain continued to come at intervals, always a little more severe than the time before. We worried and became more convinced that something was seriously wrong. But we were helpless.

Then one day, while he was taking his bath, we noticed

the bulge on his back. On his back? That was not where the pain had been! None of the doctors had paid much attention to his back, nor had it been X-rayed—the pain was always in the leg. Instinctively we knew that the worst possible thing had happened to our son. At our insistence, and after I snidely reminded him that apparently the problem had not been in my wife's head after all, the doctor immediately made an emergency appointment for us at this famous hospital two hundred and fifty miles from home. There the word *tumor* was used for the first time. There the arrangements were made for surgery in four days. We were cautioned that it could be malignant, though the surgeon assured us he had rarely seen a malignancy in a child so young and healthy. Now the day was here. . . .

We were back in the hospital long before the boy awakened. Nothing else interested us. Besides, what else matters when your child has what may be a deadly tumor?

The minutes crawled past with agonizing inertia in that crowded and smoke-filled waiting room where others waited with equal impatience. After a few hours, one lazy second reluctantly following after another, a nurse called our names and asked us to come to the pathology laboratory. With growing fear we followed her through the subterranean labyrinth. In the brightly illuminated lab we were met by a white-robed pathologist. He held a shiny basin. In it, the tumor. To my mind, that gory, red blob of tissue that had just been cut from our son's body represented evil just as the pathologist represented a priest of death. I will carry the scene with me to my grave.

Why, I wonder as I think back to that infamous day, were we informed in this way, standing in the middle of a busy corridor as if we had merely stopped to chat about the weather or Saturday's ball game? Why the basin? Why

26

make us see that killer blob? It seems so heartless and cruel.

But it was effective. A million words could not have conveyed the undisguised truth about disease and death as well as this one picture. Now, while our eyes were transfixed by that shiny, bloody basin, our ears heard only a few of the words spoken.

The pathologist was detached and cool. Why shouldn't he be, it wasn't his son. Besides, it was probably routine to him. He mentioned something about the boy still being in surgery, that the surgery was going well and should soon be completed since they were already stitching him up. He said that the tumor was malignant, *reticulum cell sarcoma* was the name he gave it, of a particularly fast-growing type that resided in and traveled through the lymph ducts, that the surgeons had not been able to remove all of it because part of the tumor was inside the spine, that the boy would almost surely die within six months. Probably much sooner.

two ⮐

We wept as the nurse led us back to Pediatrics. My wife wept openly while I, embarrassed when bypassers stared at us, tried ineffectively to hide my tears. The nurse ushered us into a little room and asked if she could send for a chaplain. The last thing I wanted to hear at that moment was pious talk about God's goodness. Whether my wife needed to talk with a chaplain I didn't stop to ask.

"Don't bother," I replied ungraciously, "I'm a minister. There's nothing he can say that we don't already know. Just leave us alone for a while."

What is it in us ministers, anyway, that makes it so difficult for us to admit we need help? Why do we pretend we can competently and successfully handle any situation? If only a fool acts as his own lawyer, then it is a bigger ignoramus who becomes his own pastor.

The nurse quickly closed the door. It was not that she was impressed by my status, I realized afterward, but rather that she had learned to recognize the anger that was slowly building up, a normal enough grief response, and decided to leave before I exploded and made her bear the brunt of it.

But I was not aware of the anger as yet. I only felt an overpowering sense of loss, as if the boy were dead already. That red blob in the shiny basin had done its fiendish work all too well. There was not a shred of doubt in my mind that the prediction was true. The boy would not recover. Nothing would ever be the same again.

My son, my precious son of whom I was so very proud, was going to die. Six months at the most, the pathologist had said, and probably much less. I did not even believe it would be six months. There was no hope whatever.

We had briefly, intellectually, considered the possibility of incurable disease and death, especially during the past four days, but we rejected it as too horrible to be real. The boy was too healthy and too active to be that seriously ill. Surely the tumor would turn out to be benign. Surely he would get better. After the surgery and period of recuperation we would take him home and all would be well once more. He would play again with his little, dependent brother who adored him and began to imitate him. No more crying about pain. No more trips to the doctor. No more frustration. Of course he would get better!

The terrible reality of the red blob shattered all those dreams and hopes beyond recovery. I leaned my head against the wall, while my wife sat in a chair. Even here, with just the two of us in the privacy of this small room and though tears still stained my face, I was not yet able to give full vent to my grief. I felt numb, as in a trance, detached from my body and my feelings. Irrationally, a vision of David flashed through my mind, and I realized there now was a sense of kinship with him as I recalled his anguished lament after the death of his beloved son, Absalom: "O my son! My son, my son! If only I had died instead of you, my son, my son!" (2 Samuel 18:33).

Move over, David! I'll join you there on the mourner's bench. So this is what it was like for you on the evening of that long-ago day when the arrows that pierced your son's heart found their mark in yours as well. How did you get through it? How will I get through it? Tell me, David! But David faded away without speaking.

Now, as I write this, I am embarrassed to admit that I cannot remember whether my wife and I touched each other at all during that agonizing hour. Surely we should have. I don't think we did, though, but I'm not sure. Perhaps some couples find comfort in shared grief, parents who are drawn to each other through strong love and common pain to support and encourage one another when something horrible happens to their child. My grief was so overwhelming that no room was left for my wife's feelings; no consoling touch, not even hers, could have taken away this sudden and excruciating sting of death. Was that selfishness, I wonder now, a sign that I did not love her then as I should have? Was it normal for me to let my hurt overshadow hers? Do other couples experience grief that way, one sitting in a chair, the other leaning against the wall? And both grieving alone?

Or was it simply an instinctive reaction beyond my control, a spontaneous withdrawal into self while every other stimulus was blocked in a feeble, frantic attempt to prevent sorrow from piling upon sorrow? The proverb may be correct in its claim that a shared sorrow is half a sorrow but only, I think, when one of those sharing has room for the sorrows of another. How can one sorrowing, shattered person really be of any help to another when the grief in his or her own cup is spilling over its brim? In the past I had known bereavement and loss, but nothing as searing and devastating as this. Perhaps because of a subconscious memory of those times, and partly because this fresh news was so painful, I temporarily shut out the world of hurt and tears, and shut out with it my wife and her pain. It was not done deliberately, consciously, but more like the body automatically turning off all of its senses to prevent an overload that could push the emotional system beyond its ability to endure. It is so very hard to handle one's own grief and to give support to one's spouse at the same time.

There is, I suppose, no right or wrong way to grieve, either as individuals or as couples. We come to our grief from our unique backgrounds. We come with different beliefs and ideals. We face life, including devastating grief episodes, out of the sum total of our past and our present. Our response is a result of who we are, where we have been, and even, I think, how often we have been in a similar situation. Our faith, our individual temperaments, our emotional pain threshold all blend together to make us act and react as the individuals we are.

I am convinced we need not apologize for our responses to pain and grief, even though we may well benefit from reflecting at some later, less stressful time on why we respond as we do. Though there may not be a right or wrong way—and surely during moments of peak stress we would be unable to distinguish them if there were—not all ways of responding are helpful. Not without reason do professionals claim statistical proof that more than four out of every five marriages end in divorce after a child dies from an incurable disease. I believe it. Few people have spiritual and emotional resources adequate for both their own survival and their spouse's. Disease kills not only persons, it can also kill relationships.

It is like two people paddling a canoe against a strong current. As long as both give their best, the canoe continues on its course. When one person grows tired, however, and slacks off a bit, a greater load falls on the other. The one who keeps rowing may become irritated. Eventually they become angry and harsh words are exchanged. The first person to drop out is now on the defensive and feels the second person should have been a bit more understanding while the second thinks the partner could have tried a little harder. Instead of understanding and empathy, they harvest anger. And meanwhile the canoe flounders on the shoals.

Cancer—that horrible, dreaded, sly killer! The word has always frightened me, like a sentence of certain and inescapable death. Already it had struck my family too often. My father, both my grandmothers, my uncle. Though some had endured for a while with lingering and increasing pain, no one had been cured. Now the death sentence was pronounced on my son.

My father was still young, only twenty-nine, when it killed him. In those days there was no antidote against cancer, nor much relief for the excruciating pain. It has always been difficult for me to accept the reality of this man's existence whose genes are duplicated in me but whom I have never seen, whose voice I have never heard, of whom I have only a few photographs. At least, I realize as I reflect on it, he had been able to marry and beget four children, though he did not live long enough to see me, his only son. But six? It wasn't fair. It was completely irrational that now my young son should be touched by this killer disease. What random, malevolent force out there picks on little children and kills them when they are only six years old?

And why did this family scourge skip over me? I had an image of my father standing on my right and my son on my left. We were as three tall evergreens standing on an open plain. Then jagged lightning flashed from heaven and the tree on my right splintered and fell to the ground. As if that were not yet enough, lightning struck again, and the tree on my left also swayed and fell over. And I alone was left, with a grief that convulsed inside me like fear. Why? Why? *Why?* My mind churned out questions to which there were no answers then and no answers now.

I walked to the window and saw that thick, threatening clouds were moving in from the southwest. It looked like rain. Involuntarily I said, "Old Jas was right. Moondogs signal change all right. Some change!"

After a while the door opened, and Sister Annemarie came in, the kind young nun who was charge nurse for the Pediatrics floor. She expressed her sympathy and asked whether we had other children. I told her about our other son, about our disappointment and pain when we learned—God, was that only two years before?—that he would be mentally impaired. She seemed sincerely touched.

"Why?" I asked her. "Why *this* child who has so much promise, who has not even begun to live? Why must he die? If we must give up a child, why not the other one who will always need supervision? Why is there now something wrong with both our boys?"

She was silent for a moment, then replied gently, "God must love you very much to ask so much of you."

My bitter response exploded out of me: "Love like that I can do without. Who needs it? I wish he'd leave us alone for a while and go love somebody else. You called this 'love'?" Now, after all these years, the words echo through my mind still, as clear as if they had just been spoken.

Like brass knuckles in a soft mitten, persistent Sister Annemarie wasn't to be denied. Her determined voice cut through my anger.

"But he does love you, you know. Both of you, and your children. Even now. Especially now. I don't know why this is happening to you either. But it is not because God doesn't love you."

I fell silent and turned to the window again. With unseeing eyes I stared at the clouds. No God there. At least I did not see him. No God here either. At least I did not feel him. My body trembled with the fury I now felt, and my hands were clenched into hard fists. The senses were beginning to work again.

Later that morning, when I had recovered from the initial shock, I began telephoning relatives with the bad news. My wife's parents; my mother and stepfather, who had just visited us and were now spending some time with my Canadian sisters; people in the church. My mother was especially shocked. Her second husband, whom she had married after being a widow for fifteen years, also had the disease and was gradually failing in health. In fact, they had been with us on that camping trip when my son's pain flared up in earnest. Everyone wanted to know whether there was something they could do. But what can be done when a little six-year-old boy has cancer? I asked an elder of my church to arrange for pulpit supply for Sunday. This was one time I could not preach.

It was well past noon before we saw our son again. He was still very sleepy, his face now pale and drawn. To me the paleness, which was nothing more than the after-effect of surgery, was the mark of death on him. He was the same child, yet no longer the same. We still had him, but in a real sense he was ours no more. The red blob in the shiny basin and the words of the pathologist stood between the past and the present. Only hours had passed since we first entered the hospital earlier this day. During those few hours, however, we had passed from a familiar, reasonably safe world into a bewildering and frightening new one.

The surgeon stopped by early in the afternoon and empathized with us. He underscored the tragic news we had already heard and reaffirmed that there was virtually no hope of recovery. Just the same, he made clear, they would initiate a series of cobalt radiation treatments within a few days, as soon as the incision had begun to heal, to bombard and possibly destroy the remaining cancer tissue that was beyond reach of the surgeon's knife. It was a chance, admittedly a slight one. But doing nothing would be to give up too soon. At least the boy had one asset: his excellent physical condition. Apart from the tumor, there was nothing wrong with him.

Big deal, I thought cynically after the man left. Apart from the tumor, nothing else matters anymore. The boy has cancer and he will most assuredly die during the time span predicted by the pathologist and the surgeon. Why cling to fragile and virtually nonexistent hope when harsh reality stares you in the face? I wasn't going to get caught up in futile dreams that would unravel within a few brief weeks. Let others torment themselves with vain hope, if they choose. Not I!

The rest of the day we took turns sitting by the bed as the boy became increasingly more alert. Nurses came at frequent intervals to check on his condition. He was doing well. The surgery had been successful. At least now we knew exactly what was going on. More than seven months of questions had received a devastating answer. But how would we tell our son? What would we tell him?

At some point during that interminable day we reached a consensus: we would not reveal anything that might possibly frighten him. Why make him live with fear and apprehension? It was enough that we knew what lay ahead. Why bother him with our burdens? We would tell him that the surgery had removed the tumor, that the radiation treatments would not hurt, that they were an attempt to make him well even faster, that the pain would perhaps not come back. We would tell him that there would be times we needed to come back to this place so the doctors could examine him to see how he was doing.

It was all the truth. But we could not tell him the whole truth, and because of that, truth really became a form of dishonesty. What else could we do? The truth was that in six months he would be dead.

How do you tell a six-year-old boy that he will die? How do you explain that this Halloween and this Thanksgiving

36

will be his last? How do you tell a little child that there will never be another Christmas after this one—how do you do it without turning even this last one into a wake instead of a celebration? How do you encourage a first grader to keep going to school when it makes no difference whether he ever learns anything again? How do you go on when life has ground to a halt?

three ❧

But of course, life did not grind to a halt. Like "Ol' Man River" it kept rolling along. No matter how heart-wrenching a given day may be, a new day , though not necessarily a better one, always comes. David can claim till he's blue in the face that "weeping may remain for a night, but rejoicing comes in the morning" (Psalm 30:5), but it isn't always so. If David were here, I would tell him that to his face. I'd remind him of his own words: "My tears have been my food day and night, while men say to me all day long, 'Where is your God?'" (Psalm 42:3). I'd tell David to quit mouthing pious promises that aren't true anyway half the time, even by his own admission. It is a refined form of cruelty to hold out hope when a situation is hopeless or to quote God's Word to one who feels God is an enemy. How can rejoicing come when you know that everything will only get worse?

For us, the day of awful discovery passed, followed by a night in which we did not sleep much. The walls in our guest house were too thin to afford much privacy. We could hear people moving around in the next room, and we knew they could hear us as well. So when we talked, we did so softly. When we wept, as we did several times during that long night, we were always conscious of those others beyond the wall.

It is hard to grieve properly when you need to consider other people. At that time, more perhaps than any other, I envied the rich. To their yachts, their luxurious homes, and fancy cars I was indifferent. These are not necessary for a good life. I was happy without any of that. But I envied their ability to afford a room in a good hotel, a room with solid walls where a man can shout or curse or pray or weep until all the emotional stress is out of his system and he regains a measure of peace. I missed, those first days after the surgery, the privacy I desperately needed. There was never an opportunity to get away from people, especially the people for whom life went on with hardly a ripple.

Still, day one after surgery was better than the one before, though it remained far from being a day of rejoicing. The boy was wide awake when we came to his room during regular visiting hours. He had wolfed down a good breakfast and could hardly wait for lunch. Although the long incision in his back caused sharp pain whenever he moved, he could not lie still for long. Being confined to bed in the middle of a perfectly good day, when there was nothing wrong with him except this pain along his spine, seemed more like punishment to him than a necessity. We insisted that he would have to stay in bed, like it or not, until the doctor said he could get up. Most of that afternoon he played with some of the small toys we had brought along or had found in the playroom at the end of the hall. Seeing those new toys made him all the more eager to get to the playroom himself. It became evident that he was not lacking in determination. He was still the firstborn, showing the characteristics that develop in children who have not an older brother or sister to imitate but make their own decisions.

We spent much of the time talking with the mother of the other boy in the room. She had traveled almost as far as we had, but from an opposite direction. Her son was about twelve, the youngest in the family, and plagued by chronic rheumatoid arthritis. He slowly shuffled in and out of the room, accompanied by pain at every move. His swollen feet could only endure soft slippers, and his hands were beginning to contract into permanently frozen claws. He would not die, at least for a long time, and not likely from the disease. While his mother felt pity for us because we would lose our son, I in turn began to think that perhaps her Mike had drawn the greater of two evils. Our son, though likely to suffer more pain before the end, would at least not suffer long.

We talked with many parents, there in Pediatrics. For some, the stay was not so bad. Their children had only minor problems and would soon return home to a normal life. But there were others. I remember one little boy with an inoperable brain tumor. The first time we saw him, he could still run through the halls. By the fourth day he was almost immobile in a wheelchair. He was promised only a few weeks of life. His parents were in agony too.

We formed instant bonds in that place, becoming a close-knit fraternity of sufferers. It reminded me of words I had read somewhere of Albert Schweitzer, the brilliant humanitarian who ministered to the sick at Lambarene in Africa, that the globe is circled by a web of pain that turns all those who suffer into brothers. There may be something to that, though the sense of affinity did not seem to come so much from the common pain as from the awareness that with these people it was not necessary to explain or justify the crazy feelings of anger and disappointment and doubt and despair. Because we had all been cast into the crucible of suffering, we quickly learned to accept and support each other and suspend judgment. Most of us were taking a new and unanticipated course in the school of life for which there had been little or no preparation. But we were

41

learning, and it was easier here than among people who have not themselves been touched by tragedy but yet think they know all about dealing with pain.

That afternoon two elders from our church surprised us with a visit. They had driven all that distance to offer their support and represent the deep concern of the congregation. They were also there to be pastors to their pastor's family—a role reversal with which they were visibly uncomfortable. Both were good men, considerably more traditional than I am, with whom on a few occasions during the past year there had been mild confrontations as I suggested changes in the life or ministry of the church that, to their great alarm, had "never been done like this before." They had come partly because they felt it was their duty as elders, but more because they genuinely cared. We talked about a number of things, skirting around the real concerns we felt. But as the time approached for them to start their five-hour trip home, they gingerly broached spiritual concerns.

One elder related how he and his wife had lost a child years ago—something I had not known. He spoke of his struggles with grief and doubt, with the question of where God had been in all that. Through that experience, one passage in the Bible had become very meaningful to him, Psalm 77. He took out his Bible and began to read. Although I never used the King James Version anymore, I nevertheless listened attentively to the old and unfamiliar words, particularly verses 7 through 9:

Will the Lord cast off for ever?
    and will he be favourable no more?
Is his mercy clean gone for ever?
    doth his promise fail for evermore?
Hath God forgotten to be gracious?
    hath he in anger shut up his tender mercies?

When the elder finished reading, he offered no answers to these troublesome questions. Instead he closed his Bible and asked his colleague to offer a prayer. Then they left. Although I was glad they had come, their coming had done more to intensify my turmoil than to bring comfort, though that was my problem and not their fault.

After supper the doctor arrived and was pleased to find the boy in good spirits. When the boy asked when he could leave the bed the doctor said that right now was fine but he could walk only within the confines of the room. Eagerly he began the attempt to get out of bed, only to wince and fall back because sharp pain flashed through him. Not to be defeated, especially before an audience, he tried again. We helped a little but he insisted he needed no help. With teeth clenched, he slid toward the edge of the bed, moved his feet over the edge, and stood up. Small beads of sweat appeared on his forehead, and his face was creased by a smile of success. He moved to the window as carefully as his roommate always did, then went to the doorway to observe activity in the hall.

Meanwhile, the doctor began to tell us about the radiation treatments that would begin in a few days. The number of treatments, he said, was not yet determined since that depended on how well the boy endured them. But they would give the maximum number of doses to do as much damage as possible to the intruding cancer cells. He cautioned that radiation also destroys healthy cells, which the body would regenerate. In the process, if all went well, the cancer cells would be defeated. He urged us again not to entertain hope of recovery. Even with the radiation therapy the outcome was dubious at best. The boy might also become nauseated or ill from the radiation. If the boy himself heard the doctor, he gave no indication.

This day, too, passed and that night we slept better. Exhaustion combined with a slight ray of hope to help relax us. We still feared the worst, yet even in fear there is always the hope that the fear will prove less threatening in reality.

The days that followed fell into a predictable routine. The boy now freely moved down the hall to the playroom where he spent hours playing with toys and other children. His incision was healing rapidly, though still quite painful the first several days. The radiation treatments began and brought with them only minimal discomfort. To all appearances, the boy's surgery had gone well. He himself began to talk of going home to play with his friends again and return to school. Being in the hospital, now that the pain was diminishing, was for him an agreeable variation in his ordinary routine. The rules under which he functioned were for the most part more relaxed than at home.

Get Well cards began arriving. How strange to receive cards with flowery, sentimental wishes that recovery would be speedy and the boy would soon be home again. All the writers knew that no recovery was promised. All knew that the boy's reprieve was only six months. Yet few mentioned that. It is so much easier to pretend all is going to be well or to hide behind the anonymity of a ready-made card than to put into words honest feelings that express real caring. Only a couple of very close friends were loving enough to confront the issue and mention they shared our pain and fears. Their words were often stumbling attempts that would never find their way onto elaborate cards, yet the scribbled notes touched us more than any card ever could.

Why is it, I often wonder, that people can be so eloquent about almost any subject, yet be at a total loss for words in the presence of grave illness or death? It isn't, I am convinced, that they do not care about those who suffer or are bereaved. Where people do not care they simply need not respond in any way, not even with a card.

Perhaps our flow of words dries up not so much because we are overcome by the suffering of the other person as by the awesome realization that it could just as well be us so afflicted. We are reminded through what happens to others of our own mortality and frailty. For all of us, life and health hang by an exceedingly thin and fragile thread.

Words may also fail us because we have the urge to say something profound and impressive. When we cannot think of a deep thought or poetic phrase we resort to the bombastic language of greeting cards, forgetting that common words can take on an eloquence far beyond their usual meaning. Ordinary words can be transformed into words of beauty when they are infused with love and caring. Of all the mail, I loved most the halting, scribbled notes because they were written from the heart.

Our son rarely concerned himself with the cards. He would look at them, ask us to read an occasional one that caught his fancy, but for the most part he ignored them. What did spark his interest were the dollar bills contained in many of the cards and letters. Although he could not yet read well, he knew that money represented the power to buy toys. To him, life was full of great and enjoyable gifts.

One day we noticed that the little boy with the brain tumor was gone, as were his parents. He had died, Sister Annemarie told us. It drove home the point again that in the midst of life we are in death, as the Book of Common Prayer says so poignantly.

Visitors came, both relatives and church members, to give visible expression of support. We became aware through their coming how important those ties of friendship or kinship can be. Though no one could feel the depth of our suffering, nor take it away, we now began to sense that when suffering is shared with those who lovingly come to stand beside the sufferers, the load seems somewhat diminished just the same. I thought of Moses, holding up his hands with the staff of God in it during that long fight with the Amelekites (Exodus 17). As long as he held his hands up, Israel was the stronger. When his arms sagged, the people fell back under the vicious attacks of the Amelekites. At the end of the day his arms were so tired he could not lift the staff any longer. Then Aaron and Hur came to hold his arms up till Israel won a decisive victory. It is a good feeling when someone cares enough to hold your hands.

I spent a week at the hospital, before returning home to take up my duties in the church. My wife stayed behind with the boy and planned to be with him until the radiation treatments were completed. Then they would both come home. By the time I left, the boy looked and acted as though he never had surgery, never had a malignant tumor, and would live forever. The picture did not square with that other picture of the red blob in the shiny basin. When I left, an undercurrent of confusion stirred beneath the ocean of despair that had never quite gone away.

four ∽

Meanwhile, what was God doing? During the elders' visit, one of them had raised questions that expressed my concerns exactly. Had God's unfailing love vanished forever? Had God forgotten to be merciful? Had he in anger withheld his compassion? These questions pressed for an answer. In the midst of my pain I didn't know the answer, nor where to look for one. I wasn't even sure there was an answer.

In all honesty, even before my son's illness I had rarely been wholly convinced of "God's unfailing love." There had been moments, to be sure, that I knew without the slightest doubt that I was God's child, that he loved me and provided for all my needs. But there had been far more times, long periods at a stretch, when I simply wondered. Occasionally I even thought the whole idea of God was no more than a figment of man's imagination, a concept concocted out of the fearful notion that it was better to have something "out there" than nothing at all. I wavered between wanting God to be kind and loving, and doubting him altogether.

Yet as a minister I was expected to talk about God, to defend both his existence and his unfailing love. I enjoyed being a minister and didn't find it difficult to represent God to this congregation that had called me to be their pastor.

47

That is mostly, I suppose, because people are so conditioned into thinking that ministers are without question "men (or women) of God." Consequently, the question is rarely even asked them: "Are you, personally, committed to God, and do you believe without doubt that you are his child?" In other words, do ministers truly believe what they preach?

I believed what I preached, and preached it honestly and without ambiguity. Only, I was not convinced that all of it applied to me personally. Theologically, I considered myself—and still do—slightly left of center, progressive, but hardly a flaming liberal. I accepted wholeheartedly the great teachings of the Bible and felt both humbled and honored that God should be willing to use me to convey biblical messages to his people, even the message that he is a faithful, loving Father. I just did not quite believe that God was *my* Father. Not that I did not want to believe it. But I could not.

My struggle went back to my childhood. I was carried to church for baptism when I was just a few weeks old. As far back as I can remember, I've gone to church at least once each Sunday—usually twice. In church and in the Christian dayschool I was taught the stories and doctrines of the Bible; Noah, Moses, David, Peter, Jesus were real people. God, too, was real most of the time. Being in church became a symbol of God's presence, and I believed he was in the midst of this congregation of which I was a part. I learned to pray. But I did not learn to love him without reservations.

Looking back, I can think of at least three reasons why I have had difficulty seeing God as loving Father. First, I grew up in a religious environment that emphasized God's sovereignty. He was the Almighty One, the Creator of heaven and earth, the one who so governs and directs our lives that we cannot even move without his will. He knows everything about us, even the number of hairs on our heads. He observes sins being committed and punishes sinners. Compared with that infinitely powerful and holy God, we puny creatures are but worms.

That could have created a great sense of belonging and security, yet there was little outward evidence of joy. That may have been, I now sometimes think, because amid all that emphasis on God's greatness and power, little was said about God's love. When it was mentioned, it was usually more an intellectual discussion than an emotional experience. God remained distant and aloof. Somehow I never realized, as I grew up and blended together all that I knew about him into my private, personal concept of God, that God wants to be known as loving Father first and as Almighty Creator last.

The second ingredient that shaped my religious understanding was that I myself did not have a father. Because he had died three months before my birth, I never experienced a father's love. The concept *father*, therefore, represented someone who was absent, who wasn't there when I needed him, someone who would never come to me again. Although I was told that he was living with Jesus in heaven, that hardly helped me here on earth. At times my mother wept because she was forced to do things my father would have done—should have done—had he not left. Sometimes I was angry with him for leaving, an irrational, childish anger, but a real anger just the same.

As I grew older, I learned that God, too, was a Father. At first it meant little, then some of the anger directed toward my father became redirected toward God. I recall standing in an open field, yellow with a glorious profusion of dandelions, when I was only six or seven and shaking my fists at God while yelling at the top of my voice, "God, I hate you for taking my dad away." It may have been faulty, this childhood perception I developed of who God

49

was and what he does, but it became ingrained in the center of my being. If, ultimately, for all of us the God whom we worship is a God of our own making—a combination of what we have been taught and what we have observed—my God became one who is neither kind nor dependable but one who is distant and absent. It is difficult to feel love for him whom you have at times hated, one to whom you have never felt close.

The third aspect has to do with the occupation of my country by the Nazis. The all-pervasive fear and insecurity that gripped most adults at that time was transmitted in subtle, usually nonverbal ways to children. We were taught never to trust strangers, particularly authority figures who carried guns. It was permissible to lie to them, a virtue far greater than telling the truth. You only trusted those whom you knew very, very well. It is easy to learn how to mistrust. It comes almost naturally. After that, trust becomes a formidable challenge, one with which I had only limited success. God too was a stranger, someone with whom my personal encounters had only been few and infrequent. Intellectually, I knew all about him. Emotionally, I kept him at arm's length.

So it continued while I moved from being a child to being a man, from the old world to the new, despite occasional reassuring episodes where the Holy Spirit spoke to me and I knew it to be him—that I was God's child and that he loved me. But by that time I had become comfortable with God's distance and my independence. As a young adult I made a profession of faith, expressed my commitment to Christ, and became a member in full fellowship of my church. But to what the head testified, the heart did not always express agreement.

When I learned my son would die, what I knew intellectually about God gave way to what I had always felt about him in the secret recesses of my soul. All my old, angry feelings about God surfaced. Some had been barely laid to rest after the turmoil two years earlier when we learned our second boy was mentally impaired. Questions without number spawned in my mind. What kind of vicious God is this anyway, who first takes away a little boy's father when the little boy is not even born and then bides his time until the boy becomes a father himself, only to take away this new father's little boy? How can God cause so much pain and then, when you finally think things are improving, come back and do it all over again, not once but twice?

I wrestled with the words of Jesus in the Sermon on the Mount (Matthew 7:9–11): "Which of you, if his son asks for bread, will give him a stone? Or if he asks for a fish, will give him a snake? If you, then, though you are evil, know how to give good things to your children, how much more will your Father in heaven give good things to those who ask him!"

Try though I might, I perceived only stones and snakes, and could not decide whether that meant I was not good and had all of this coming or whether God was not good. The question was not, "Where now is God?" I knew where he was all along, safely enthroned in heaven and untouched by my pain. The question became, "Where now is *my* God?" And the answer came back loudly, "Just when you need him, he's not there. Don't count on him." I envied Wanderhope, the grieving father in Peter DeVries' touching novel, *The Blood of the Lamb,* who, after his little girl died, dared express his angry contempt for God by plastering a cake over the face of a crucifix. But when God hides cowardly behind distance and silence, how can you throw a pie in his face?

"Call upon me in the day of trouble; I will deliver you," God said a long time ago (Psalm 50:15). "For everyone who asks, receives; he who seeks finds; and to him who knocks, the door will be opened" (Matthew 7:8). That's what Jesus promised. But try calling when you stand next to the bed of a little boy who will be dead in six months, and you hear only silence. Approach God and you hear the great doors of heaven swing shut and the deadbolts slide into their sockets. Look for a doorknob and you find there is none. Knock on the door until your knuckles are raw and bleeding, pound until your arms feel as though they are about to fall out of their sockets, but you'll hear no footsteps on the other side of that door, though at times you think there is an eye watching you from the spyglass. Ask, beg, plead, cajole, and it will all be equally ineffective.

Why is it that God only speaks in church when the organ plays or in a forest when the sun shines and cardinals sing, but never in a hospital or a funeral home? Why is it that he hounds us, like a terrier yapping at our heels, when we want to be left alone, but is never there when we so desperately need him?

With C. S. Lewis I could say, back in the weeks after the boy's surgery when I was so brutally hurt and still so terribly angry, "Not that I am (I think) in much danger of ceasing to believe in God. The real danger is of coming to believe such dreadful things about him. The conclusion I dread is not 'So there is no God after all,' but 'So this is what God's really like. Deceive yourself no longer.' "[1]

Fruitlessly, I wrestled with the Herculean task of reconciling the conclusions reached about God during my childhood and so harshly reaffirmed in the things that happened to my sons, with all the tantalizing promises that God makes in the Bible. So many Christians seem to accept these promises without any difficulty whatever, while to me they seemed to be only hollow and hypocritical platitudes. While my habit of regular personal prayer in the past was only weak at best, now I could not pray at all, at least not for myself. I felt that God was callously playing with my emotions, and I became convinced that his play was dead serious, deliberate, malicious.

In time, the boy and his mother came home. Our lives resumed a semblance of normalcy once more. After seventeen cobalt treatments, the doctors had decided that this was the maximum dose his body could endure. They told us that he would not be able to have any more radiation in the future. They still held out no greater hope for a cure, despite the boy's remarkable recovery from the surgery and effects of radiation. He received no medications and apparently needed none. The pain was now completely gone, and the boy looked once more a picture of radiant health. Only the livid scar on his back reminded us of the tumor that had lodged there until so very recently. That, and the appointments at the hospital every two or three weeks for checkups and blood tests. So began our routine of trips back and forth between home and the hospital.

Still, we lived in the expectation of death. We visited a photographer. The four of us who as yet formed a family posed for a portrait. How easy it was to freeze time in this way, to sit on a bench together, say "cheese," and in a few weeks have reproduced on a piece of paper the permanent image of a model family. Outwardly, the portrait turned out so beautifully, all of us in our Sunday best and the boy in the new sport coat my wife had just sewn for him. What the camera did not capture was the inward pain behind our smiles, the anxious realization that this would not last, that what we tried to make permanent was only temporary and all too fleeting. It was a charade; in reality we were trying to make peace with approaching death.

We also had the boy pose alone. Not knowing why he was singled out, he enjoyed the experience. His pictures, like ours, turned out splendidly. Nevertheless, looking at

53

them now, I detect on his face a pensive look as though unconsciously he was already aware there would be very little opportunity for pictures in the future.

Meanwhile, while time so slowly passed, I continued to carry out all the things expected of a minister. Though I could no longer pray for myself, I prayed eloquently for others, but never publicly for my son. Despite my persistent doubts about the goodness and love of God, each week I prepared and preached two sermons that gave no hint of my struggle. I conducted funerals where I spoke in glowing terms about the bright hope we have and the glorious future that awaits God's people while for my personal future I saw nothing but darkness and pain. In church education classes I said all the expected things even when at times I felt a strong urge to curse God and turn my back on him. It was hypocritical and deceitful, a holy masquerade fueled by tradition and unrealistic expectations. Sometimes I envied my wife. She at least did not have to feel one thing and say another because people expected something positive. But, of course, she had her own private struggles too.

We could have used a pastor during this time, my wife and I, but we had none. I had no pastor because I was the pastor, and pastors walk hand in hand with God so that they need no pastoral care themselves. Or so the church often reasons. And so also pastors, including me, frequently reason. I made no attempt to seek out anyone's support, nor did anyone approach me. I had many good friends, some of them pastors themselves, but I kept even from them much of my agony. Nor did my wife have a pastor; all she had was a husband who was no pastor to her nor, even now, much of a husband. We shared little, and even that was rather superficial. I simply could not tell her about my growing doubt and despair.

I now know something that I did not realize then;

namely, that it is not God who plays with our emotions but Satan. Like he toyed with Job—with God's incomprehensible permission—during that terrible wager he struck with God that Job would prove less loyal than God thought, so Satan played with me on the assumption that I would not endure. I think of what Helmut Thielicke has written:

> The tempter is a good psychologist. . . .
>
> And so the tempter, when he proposes to attack in earnest, allows the suffering to exceed the limits of what a man can regard as reasonable. The moment at which he [man] thinks it must stop because he has learned enough is precisely the moment at which it does not cease; it goes on senselessly. Time is the most uncanny minister of this prince of darkness. Time saps our resistance. Not because it goes on so long, but because it is so meaningless, and because suffering which goes on and on turns into a grotesquely scornful question: "What do you say now?" "Where is now thy God?" (Psalm 42:3). "Do you still think this suffering is sent by God? What sense do you see in it? How can it still, after all these months and years, 'be for your good'?" "Are you really still holding on to your piety—and for how much longer?" "Curse God and die" (Job 2:9). . . .
>
> At bottom he does nothing but play upon man's natural attitude towards God and push it to its furthest extreme. He simply makes use of the qualities of human nature . . . he leads man with the aid of time—i.e., with the aid of long-continued suffering—to a point at which man can no longer see any sense in his sufferings, and certainly cannot understand how they can give him maturity and help him on his way. This is the point at which, with diabolical inevitability, his belief in God appears absurd, and he abjures God.[2]

It was about this time that a lady in our neighborhood, no doubt thinking herself God's messenger, came to talk to us about the problem of unconfessed sin in our life. That is another aspect of suffering, usually noticed only by those on the receiving end. Suddenly there is a whole class of people who interpret their own untouched state as a divine mandate to bring the afflicted ones to repentance. Instead of giving thanks for having escaped illness or tragedy, and praying that it may remain so, they become busybodies who through letters, crank phone calls, or personal visits torment those struggling with pain. They have an arrogance, these self-styled "agents of the Almighty," that is offensive yet hard to counter.

Paul Tournier has written the following about them:

> The misfortune is that all men claim to express, through their own judgments, the judgment of God Himself. It is an absolutely universal phenomenon. Men make a monopoly of God, even those who do not believe in Him, but especially those who wish to serve Him and lead men to Him. When they judge the conduct of others, they all do it in a peremptory manner, implying that God Himself could not judge them otherwise. They are so strongly convinced in their opinion of what is good and evil that it seems to them that God would betray Himself if He did not share their opinion.[3]

Like Job's friends, who never quite understood the agony behind Job's words, so these people barely understand what they say themselves and nothing of what the afflicted one says in return. Our neighbor, though she spoke to my wife and me together, was really addressing me.

"Pastor," she said, sincerely and obviously taken with her own good intentions, "God does not do these things to your children without reason. You must have some unacknowledged and unconfessed sin in your life. I beg of you, please repent, go to God, and ask for his forgiveness. He will cleanse you from your sin and heal your children."

In a totally uncharacteristic and unpastoral response, I refused to listen and asked her to leave, at once, which she did. But her words lingered. What if she was right? What if these things were punishment? Would God do something like that? To which my answer came back: Yes, God probably would.

Six months after the boy's surgery, when, according to the predictions of the pathologist and the surgeon, he should have been dead, he was in better health than ever. His checkups at the hospital found no trace of cancer, either by X-ray or through blood tests. It was too good to be true, and I waited for the other shoe to drop. Meanwhile I still wrestled with the overwhelming and unresolved questions of God's involvement in our lives. Nothing made sense anymore; I questioned our purpose for living. The words of the old confession that the chief end of man is to "love God and enjoy him forever" no longer comforted or encouraged me. By contrast, Nietzsche's words, "He who has a *why* to live for can bear with almost any *how,*" became fulfilled in my life—in a negative sense.

On Good Friday, I intended to preach on John 3:16, "For God so loved the world that he gave his one and only Son, that whoever believes in him shall not perish but have eternal life." As I worked on the sermon, I suddenly reached the point where I could not say another word about God's love. It seemed nothing but sheer hypocrisy to mouth platitudes about a love that I questioned and of which I felt nothing. I could not defend the indefensible. I could not speak about eternal life since I still believed my son would die. The stress, the fatigue, the pain and uncertainty, however, all combined to push me beyond my limits. In an outburst of angry despair, I tore up the half-completed sermon and vowed never to make another as long as I live. My response was a modern-day fulfillment of Solomon's astute observations that "hope deferred makes the heart sick" (Proverbs 13:12) and "heartache crushes the spirit" (Proverbs 15:13). It had taken a while for the effects to become visible, but now I had indeed reached the point of being crushed.

That Good Friday I did not preach. Nor on Easter, for on that day I began the long trip to a private psychiatric hospital to sign myself in as a patient. Suddenly I needed healing more than my son.

five 〰

I stayed at the hospital nearly two months. Because the distance made visits difficult, I saw my two boys not at all and my wife only once or twice during that period. For all of us it was yet another upheaval in our family life, yet another weakening of the increasingly fragile bonds that held us together. Absence may make the heart grow fonder, but not necessarily of home. Long and repeated periods of separation are more likely to diminish than enhance the cohesion within a family. We all licked our wounds, in different ways, in different places, and tragically alone. I sometimes wonder whether in the long run the cure was more harmful than the disease. I doubt I would advise anyone to seek therapy so far away from home, no matter how excellent the facility may be.

For me it was a letting go, first of all, of the responsibilities connected with pastoring a congregation. How can anyone lift up another if he himself is worn out? How can he point the way to God if he himself doesn't know where God is hiding? How can he help someone's faith grow if his own is embattled by doubt? How can he comfort if his own emotions are torn to shreds?

It was also a letting go of the burden of my son's illness. Sure, the concern stayed with me. But at least I did not have to look at him each day and wonder why he was still alive when we had been told he would soon die. I did not have to ask myself, each time he came through the door, when would be the last time.

Therapy became a process of painful healing and personal growth. My roommate taped a huge poster on our door that said, "A friend is someone who knows all about me and loves me anyway." For the first time in my life I began to learn, though at a snail's pace, what trust is. Though it was difficult, I began to open up to a counselor, to reveal some of my fears, to share my frustration and my pain.

Intense personal counseling is like peeling an onion. The outer layer of dry husk comes off relatively easily. It is a protective cover only, not really part of the onion anymore and certainly not edible. No one is much interested in the husk. The second layer is more reluctant to let go. Now one is dealing with the onion itself, even though parts of this layer may already be drying up and turning into a protective husk. Once this layer is removed, the onion lies there open and undefended. Continue peeling, layer after layer—there are so many layers to an onion—and tears begin to flow. You cannot peel onions— or undergo serious counseling—without weeping.

I wept, in those weeks, as I came to know myself better, as I reflected on who I was, where I had come from, and what went into making me the person I was. With the counselor's help, I faced my grief over my son's illness and coming death, along with the unresolved feelings over my other son's retardation. I learned that it is permissible for a man to cry, that the tough macho act behind which I had long hidden, just as so many other men do, is neither helpful nor honest. Men need to release their emotions just as women do. Bottled-up feelings are like a pressurized tank. If there is no occasional release of the tension, eventually the tank will explode. Explosions almost always cause injury to the people standing near the tank, and they don't do the tank any good either.

It was a cleansing experience, being in that hospital, a period of rebuilding my inner strength, of coming to grips with the reality that life is often unfair and painful but that adjusting to life is healthier than fighting against it. But it was only a beginning; the real test comes in everyday situations where people wrestle with questions about their work, their purpose, and God's involvement in their lives.

The accusation of the neighbor lady continued to fester within me. She had unwittingly touched a tender nerve. During those painful months I felt I was under some secret curse, as though God had withdrawn his protection from me and I stood defenseless against whatever he chose to send next. I wondered whether my sons were afflicted because of some sin I had committed. The awful thought would not go away that perhaps this was God's way of getting even. The neighbor's words reaffirmed my doubts and fears and, I felt, represented the thinking of others that there is a direct connection between sin and sickness, specifically my sin and the afflictions of my two sons.

These guilt feelings also caused friction between my wife and me. We wondered whether what happened to our children was our fault. It is a heavy burden, this thought that perhaps everything would be different had we lived better lives. I did not know then that almost all parents whose children are incurably ill or disabled have these feelings and go through this struggle. After a while, when the load gets too heavy, one spouse begins to blame the other. If one spouse can somehow determine that the cause rests with the other or is the result of a genetic flaw that runs in the family of the other, then that spouse can forego responsibility in the matter. It is a destructive process, this blame-seeking, that undermines personal confidence and destroys trust within marriages. Guilt, however unrealistic and undeserved it may be, makes individuals behave strangely.

Most churches of the denomination to which I then belonged have the habit of reading the Ten Commandments every Sunday morning. God clearly says that he is "a jealous God, punishing the children for the sin of the fathers to the third and fourth generation of those who hate me" (Exodus 20:5). I wondered whether God really punishes parents through their little children. Again, the image flashed through my mind of the little boy at the hospital who had died so quickly after his brain tumor had been discovered. It seemed irrational that God should make war on little boys like him and like my son. Reconciling that with the biblical description of God as a loving and compassionate Father became impossible.

David also came to mind. After his adultery with Bathsheba, Nathan the prophet came to rebuke David. David was told that the little baby that Bathsheba had just brought into the world would die as a direct consequence of their sin (2 Samuel 12:14). Was that, I agonized, why one son is retarded and the other incurably ill? But what was my sin? If I was being punished for sin, shouldn't God be more specific, shouldn't he spell out clearly what my transgression had been? I could not remember any particular, unusually grave sin that either my wife or I had committed. Ours were merely the normal, garden variety little sins common to most Christians. What good is punishment, I reasoned, if it is indefinite, if there is no clear connection between the transgression and its consequences? At least David knew why his boy died; shouldn't God at least have the decency to tell me why mine would die?

Then I remembered Job. He was a good man. God boasted about him to Satan: "Have you considered my servant Job? There is no one on earth like him; he is blameless and upright, a man who fears God and shuns evil" (Job 1:8). Despite Job's goodness and loyalty to God, one day the orderly, enjoyable world of this man crumbled as messengers came, one after the other, to tell him that his possessions and his children were gone. Some time after that, Job himself was afflicted with a painful, devastating illness. When his friends came to console him, they found him on the garbage heap, so totally changed through pain and grief that they could hardly recognize him. Job had done no wrong; in fact, he was so conscientious in his devotion to God that he sacrificed burnt offerings for his children whenever he feared they had cursed God in the secrecy of their hearts. What an admirable man, this Job, and what a faithful servant of God! Yet even the life of this righteous man dissolved into a whirlpool of pain that threatened to engulf him and swallow him up.

Job wrestled with his friends over the question of how suffering relates to sin. Like the friends, he had always believed that sickness and misfortune were visible proofs that sinful misconduct had resulted in divine punishment. The friends, because they remained untouched, saw no reason to revise their theology. Job, however, remaining unshakably convinced of his own noble conduct and innocence, now realized that the old way of thinking was all wrong. Suffering can come, and often does, when no sin has been committed. Consequently, Job and his friends argued past each other in their interminable discourses. They were not addressing the same issue. The friends remained sure Job had sinned, and so they tried to lead him to a point of confession and forgiveness. Job, on the other hand, pleaded with God and wanted God to lift his unfair and undeserved punishment.

Job also realized how unreasonable it is to think that God actually punishes a man through his children. He said, "It is said, 'God stores up a man's punishment for his sons.' Let him repay the man himself, so that he will know it! Let his own eyes see his destruction; let him drink of the wrath of the Almighty" (Job 21:19–20).

Had Job known the passage, he would have appealed to and agreed with Ezekiel:

> "What do you people mean by quoting this proverb about the land of Israel:
> 'The fathers eat sour grapes,
> and the children's teeth are set on edge'?
> "As surely as I live, declares the Sovereign Lord, you will no longer quote this proverb in Israel. For every living soul belongs to me, the father as well as the son—both alike belong to me. The soul who sins is the soul who will die. . . .
> "The son will not share the guilt of the father, nor will the father share the guilt of the son." (18:2–4, 20)

Though this passage brought me a measure of peace by removing the guilt of personal responsibility, it did not provide an explanation why these troubles had come to our family. I tried to balance texts like Hebrews 12:6, "The Lord disciplines those he loves," with Lamentations 3:33, "For he does not willingly bring affliction or grief to the children of men." Unlike a mathematical equation, however, the texts did not add up or resolve anything. And I was unable—unwilling, too—simply to sit back and accept what was happening as "God's will." How can illness and death ever be God's will when one of the reasons Jesus came was to show through his miracles that God wants health and wholeness for his people? More and more I turned to the comfort and assurance of Revelation 21:4, 5. *That*, I knew, was truly descriptive of God's will: "'He will wipe every tear from their eyes. There will be no more death or mourning or crying or pain, for the old order of things has passed away.' He who was seated on the throne said, 'I am making everything new!'"

More and more, I began to accept what was happening to my children as the random consequence of life in a disrupted and hostile creation, where sin in its many forms has warped or destroyed the good life God had envisioned for his children. A long sentence from a liturgical form used at times of baptism came to mind:

> For when we are baptized into the Name of the Father, God the Father witnesses and seals unto us that He makes an eternal covenant of grace with us and adopts us for His children and heirs, and therefore will provide us with every good thing and *avert all evil or turn it to our profit.*[4]

I had read the sentence many times. Now it took on a new and comforting meaning all its own. Increasingly I knew that my neighbor had been wrong. What happened to my sons was not a punishment for my sin. Besides, I reasoned, how could God punish in my sons those sins that he had already punished once before when Jesus died on the cross of Golgotha to make atonement for all God's children, including me? Surely, God is not so grossly unfair as to exact payment for sin twice over.

Suddenly the truth dawned. If what happened to my sons was the punishment for my sins, the atonement accomplished by Christ had been incomplete and inadequate, which would make his triumphant cry, "It is finished," a lie. But God does not lie, nor does Christ. Thus, when Jesus said it was finished, that meant no one would ever have to make payment for sin again to satisfy the demands of God's justice. Relief flooded through me and I felt like singing. I was getting ready to face the world again, even though much more time was needed to complete the process of growth that had now begun. Hesitantly, I began to draw closer to God and trust him ever so slightly. There really was no choice. Turning away from God could only point me in a direction of total disaster and hopelessness.

A few days later, just before I left the hospital, the chaplain approached me to stimulate possible interest I might have in hospital chaplaincy. The thought had sometimes crossed my mind, but only briefly. He encouraged me very strongly to consider this important ministry to people in pain. He reinforced his argument with the simple statement: "You would be sensitive to people because you know what it is like to bleed."

Though I knew how to bleed and was beginning to learn how to weep when painful events happened, I was not ready for the transition from congregational ministry to hospital chaplaincy. Not then, at any rate. How could I force my family to go through yet another upheaval when there was so much uncertainty already? It would take more time and a great deal more convincing.

When I went home, my son was up to all his old activities as though nothing had ever happened to him. He played hard and slept without being interrupted by pain. If it were not for the angry scar an inch to the left of his lower spine, the whole episode would have been written off as nothing but a horrible nightmare that had passed. Yet the scar reminded us: the tumor had indeed been there.

We continued to visit the hospital at regular intervals. Each time, the doctors seemed more optimistic as they performed their tests and took X-rays. Everything they saw suggested that our son was in excellent health once more—not a sign of a tumor nor a trace of abnormal cells in his blood. Gradually the time between checkups lengthened. The doctors began to use the words "remission" and "cure," though always with some reservations. They did not want us to entertain unfounded hopes. Yet with the passing of the months, hope began to replace fear in our hearts. Perhaps a miracle had happened. Perhaps our son would live.

Through all these months we continued to receive assurances from friends all over the country that they were regularly praying for us and for our son. I had been unable to pray at first when the news of the tumor was still reverberating through my soul. Now, as hope took root, I dared plead with God again: "Lord, come down; my son is ill. If you but speak, he will be healed. Show your power and your love. Make all things well again."

With such an outpouring of prayer and the assurance in the book of James that the prayers of the righteous are powerful and effective, how could God fail to take note? While I dared make no claim that I was deserving of being called righteous, I knew many of those who prayed with us had strong faith. Where I sometimes doubted, they were unshakably convinced that petitions asked in faith and offered in Christ's name would invariably be answered.

Month followed month like an ever-brightening string of precious pearls. More and more, we became convinced that God had answered prayers. A year passed, then a year-and-a-half. Now we were sure the cancer cells were all dead, and the boy was still invigoratingly alive. God was good to us. We had been plunged into the abyss of despair, but God had reached down and lifted us out. As he had done with Abraham on Mount Moriah, he had restored to us from death the son we loved so much, a gift now doubly precious because we had already adjusted ourselves, more or less, to having to give him up. Now we had him back. Now we would be privileged to see him grow up. My wife and I rejoiced. Our friends praised God with us.

I began to feel guilty over my earlier negative, hostile

thoughts about the God who turned out to be, after all, loving and compassionate. So this, I thought, is what a father is like. When you need him the most, when you can't do something without the help of someone stronger and bigger, God is there, ready to help. All you have to do is ask and he responds. I lived those days with a warm glow in my heart about the God whom I was at long last beginning to trust as my heavenly Father. There was hope again, bright hope for tomorrow. Sure, we had wept, but the weeping had only lingered for a while. Now was the dawn of a new day. The tears had been replaced by smiles.

We returned to the hospital once more. The doctor was so delighted and impressed by the boy's condition that he decided to call the surgeon.

"In this business," said the doctor, "we have a lot of disappointments. It is encouraging, for a change, to see a patient who will make it, especially one with this type of cancer."

The surgeon was equally pleased, though he cautioned us not to consider the boy cured until at least two years had passed without any recurrence of symptoms. They looked at the results of the blood tests and X-rays; all were positive and encouraging. We went home, buoyed up and reassured as never before. We shared the good news with our friends and took time to thank God. Surely the Lord was good!

Two weeks later, the boy complained about pain in his leg and we saw that the tell-tale bulge was back again, right where it had been the first time.

six 〰

"God, where are you? Are you as shocked as I am that the bulge is back? Or did you know all along it would come? Did you plan for it to come back?

"I need to pray, I try to pray. But I have a hard time praying. I try to think of you, and I can't think of you without feeling betrayed, let down when I trusted you, when I praised you for your goodness.

"Tonight I feel so engulfed by pain and bitterness that it's like a noose choking off my words and my thoughts.

"I can't sleep. When I went for a walk tonight, it did not relax me the way it usually does. My heart was a lump of ice in my chest, a heavy spot so cold that pain radiated through my whole chest. All my attempts to think positive thoughts failed. I could only think of that bulge that has returned to the boy's back, that killer we thought was gone for good.

"The stars sparkled so brightly in the dark sky this evening. At other times I stand in awe of those countless stars and planets you have scattered through the universe. They remind me of your majesty and greatness, your wisdom and love. The constellations that have guided sailors for centuries testify to your faithfulness, for they are always in the same place, dependable and trustworthy.

Tonight it seemed as though their twinkling was a mockery. Your majesty was not a comfort but a threat.

"Why, if you are so great and powerful and loving, did you not prevent the tumor from coming back? How can you just sit in your heaven and let it happen? Don't you know how much we hurt? Don't you care what's happening to us? Didn't you know I was just beginning to trust you and feel close to you? Why did you have to go and spoil it all again?

"The house is quiet now. My wife must at last have fallen asleep. A while ago I heard her cry in the room upstairs. I did not go to her. What can I say that will make her pain go away? What can she say to make mine less? God, why is there always something to drive us apart again?

"And now what are we going to tell the boy? How can we explain to him that you want him dead instead of alive? How can we convince him that you love him when you are determined to kill him? And why does he have to die when he has a little brother who needs him so much, who adores him and imitates him? Don't we have enough pain?

"I trusted you. I really trusted you. I was so sure that you would hear the prayers, if not mine then at least those of my friends. You said so. You promised you would give what we asked for, you would answer when we called. We thought you had answered when the disease went into remission. We thanked you for it. And now look what happened to the promises! Talk it is, all talk and no substance! Cheap words without foundation! You're nothing but a big blabbermouth. How can we ever believe you? When do you mean what you say?

"The ticking of the clock echoes loudly through this room. 'You fool! You fool! You fool! You fool!' That's what it sounds like. And that's how I feel. How could I be so dumb to get my hopes up? I know that cancer is a killer. It grabs and never lets go again. It is never satisfied with anything less than death. It is like you. You never let go either.

"Why don't you just turn your back and leave me alone. At least then I'd have some peace for a while—until the boy dies or I die. Why did you have to raise our hopes if all along you knew they would be crushed again? Why did you give the boy a remission if you already planned he would not get better anyway?

"I knew it! I knew it! I knew all along that the boy would not live. Why then did I hope? To hope for anything where cancer is involved is sheer idiocy. Better to be realistic and live only in the present. Accept what you have and don't dream about things that may never become reality. How dare I ever again let my heart rule over reason? Solomon was right. 'Joy may end in grief,' he wrote (Proverbs 14:13). It always does. And you do nothing to stop it.

"Have I done something wrong again? Is this your way of getting even once more? Are you saying to me,

Since you rejected me when I called
    and no one gave heed when I stretched out my
        hand,
since you ignored all my advice
    and would not accept my rebuke,
I in turn will laugh at your disaster;
    I will mock you when calamity overtakes you—
when calamity overtakes you like a storm,
    when disaster sweeps over you like a whirlwind,
    when distress and troubles overwhelm you.

Then they will call to me but I will not answer;
    they will look for me but will not find me.
        (Proverbs 1:24–28)

71

"Is that what's happening to me?

"God, talk to me! Help me make some sense out of all this.

"How can I let him go? I love him so much. He's everything I've ever hoped for. With him gone, nothing will ever quite matter again. I beg you, Lord, grant me the life of my son.

"I need you, God. I need your help, we all need your help, now more than ever. How will we ever get through the months ahead? How will we tell the boy and prepare him for what's going to happen? Please God, do something. Don't let us struggle all alone. If you love us, like you say you do, show us, for Jesus' sake!"

That night there was no word from the Lord. No Spirit spoke to console me. No angels came to minister to me. There was just the clock, ticking away the endless minutes. That, and my tears flowing freely in the silence.

Eventually came the dawn. But the morning brought no joy. And the bulge was still there.

seven ≋

As quickly as possible we returned to the hospital. The doctors were as disappointed as we were. Though they had said, eighteen months earlier, that the boy could have no more radiation, a new series of treatments was started. The reason was clear. Without any treatment, he was doomed. With treatment, there was a chance, however remote, of a second remission. In their decision they walked the tightrope between certain death and possible death—a horrible dilemma.

The boy was by now aware something was drastically amiss. This was no ordinary, routine visit. There was little of the lighthearted bantering that the doctors had engaged in in the past and which he always enjoyed. Instead the mood now was one of determination to fight the tumor with every weapon available in the medical arsenal. He stayed with his mother in yet another boardinghouse near the hospital while the treatments ran their course. In another situation it would have been like a vacation. Like a typical boy, he did not mind having all this extra time off. As for my wife, she handled bravely the lonely task of living temporarily in a strange town with a little boy who talked about all the things he would do when he grew up while all along she knew, but could not tell him, that none of those things could ever be. In some sense she shouldered, more than I, the real burden of the boy's illness just like women all through history have diligently borne domestic burdens for which they received little praise while their husbands meanwhile went about their glorious tasks of being men.

After the radiation came chemotherapy. The deadly poisons were slowly dripped into the boy's veins, a small dose each day, in the hope that they would seek out and destroy the malignant cells before these had a chance to kill the boy himself. This was something he did not like. It was not only the pain. After a few days, he became familiar enough with the routine to know what to expect. Bravely he suffered through the injections and the daily attempts to find a vein. What bothered him more was the possibility that he would lose his hair. He had overheard an unfortunate chance remark to that effect when two nurses talked together about another patient and thought they were talking about him. He was right, to be sure. Hair loss was one of the possible side effects of chemotherapy. To us, having a bald son was a small price to pay if it would keep him alive. He did not know what was at stake because we had not yet told him. And so the hair became an object of major concern to him.

The hair did not fall out. For that he was grateful. Nor did the tumor diminish. It bulged beneath the incision on his back that now looked even more threatening, stretched as it was by the alien tissue. The danger was not that the skin would rupture but rather that the cancer cells would begin to travel through the lymph ducts and settle in other parts of the body, especially the vital organs. The pathologist had already mentioned that possibility when the boy had surgery months before. To our relief it had not yet happened. Just the same, the threat loomed large.

That spring was a caldron of intense and often conflicting emotions. We welcomed the end of a long winter that had been more severe than most. Repeated blizzards had dumped so much snow on the region that nearly half the roads were permanently closed. Slowly the thick snow pack disappeared. Some flooding occurred. Everywhere flowers appeared and a hush of fresh green replaced the ugly brown spots between the lingering mountains of snow. Robins returned along with other songbirds to sing their praises to the great Creator. New life appeared on branches that for so many months had seemed totally lifeless. It was a period of optimism and new hope all through God's marvelous creation.

Yet all this beauty was overshadowed by the ever-growing cloud of doom that hung over the boy. The happy songs of the birds in the trees just outside our kitchen windows found no echo in our hearts. As we looked at the flowers and the delicate shades of green leaves, we could only wonder whether the boy would still be alive when the leaves turned brown and the flowers froze with the first autumn frost. Would he rest beneath the soil when the snows returned? And, before that time came, what would happen to him? And to us?

We wrestled with the dreadful question of whether to tell him he was dying. He was only seven years old. Children have such limited understanding of death. He had not really begun thinking in abstractions as yet; everything was still concrete to him. On the one hand we wanted to be honest with him, just as we had always urged him to be honest with us. But we had never anticipated that honesty could become a matter of life and death, *his* life and death. How could we tell him about death when he possibly would not understand? How could we voice something that could frighten him and perhaps interfere with the healing process? Does a seven-year-old have a right to know? Does he need to know? Is it good for him to know? There were no easy answers to the painful questions. In the end, we chose not to tell him for the time being. Perhaps God would yet remember to be gracious and heal him. Why frighten the boy before all hope of recovery was gone? It was an uneasy decision to which we saw no better alternative.

About this time, we were deluged by all sorts of unsolicited advice on how to cure cancer. Several people called or wrote letters claiming that the medical establishment was suppressing proven cures, many of them astonishing in their simplicity. The reason given was invariably the doctors' greed. If cancer patients were cured so easily, doctors would no longer make the enormous amounts they now collected from their patients. There were herbs, fruit juices, and special diets that had cured, so it was claimed, many cancer patients who had the courage to defy the establishment and take their healing into their own hands.

Naturally skeptical, we rejected most of the advice as old-wives' tales and quackery. Still, we were desperate. We needed to be convinced that we had tried everything and had left no possible chance untouched. How vulnerable we were then, I now realize, and such easy prey for people who perhaps meant well but more likely pounced on their victims because it gave them a temporary sense of importance. We should have seen through them but we didn't.

In time our resolve weakened. We fell victim to the urge to try anything, no matter how bizarre. It is common enough, I now know, for desperate parents to fall into this trap. We took the boy to a man who could supposedly diagnose disease and suggest a curative course of action simply by looking into a patient's eyes. He did not even diagnose that the boy had cancer. We came away disillusioned and feeling foolish. After that, we tried someone's grape juice cure. For a few days we made the boy drink enormous amounts of unsweetened grape juice because, as an article that someone showed us claimed, it supposedly cured cancer. When the boy became rebellious at the sight of still more juice, we came to our senses.

"If he is going to die, let's let him die," I said to my wife. "But we're not going to make his last days a grape-juice hell."

How we dreaded the coming months and how futile seemed our attempts to save the boy! Almost constantly he complained about pain. As at the beginning of his ordeal, the center of pain was always in his upper left leg. The doctors explained it by saying that the tumor pressed on the nerves in the lower spine, just where they branched into separate bundles for each leg. Like sound travels along a water pipe to become audible far from its source, so the pain coursed almost two feet along the nerves until becoming localized in one throbbing spot. Pain pills had only minimal impact. The boy learned to cry again, especially in his sleep. We learned the meaning of frustration when nothing we tried had any effect on the pain. As he whimpered in his sleep, we began to sit with him to rub his leg and head, the touch of our hands more consoling for him than soothing. At least we were there, though no one could soothe our heartache. For us there was no balm.

Occasionally someone would try to comfort or encourage us by reaffirming that God makes no mistakes, that nothing happens without his will, that all of this was part of some wonderful plan he has for our lives. For me, those assurances crumbled each time I stood beside my son's bed as he cried in his sleep or when I saw him walk across the lawn with that slight limp that was just becoming noticeable. People stopped to quote Romans 8:28 to us, invariably in the King James Version: "And we know that all things work together for good to them that love God, to them who are called according to his purpose." The way they put it was as if to say that cancer in a little boy is a good thing, that we should give thanks to God for doing all this for us, that we should realize this was a sign of God's enduring love, living proof that he was working to make us better people.

The words brought no comfort. It was impossible at that time for us to see any good in this catastrophe. Those glib words that rolled off people's tongues still left us with a little boy who was dying while the comforters could return home to their healthy children and their undisturbed lives. How easy it is to give advice from the security of one's own safe and untouched position to someone struggling to keep from drowning. And how hollow the advice sounds when it is not forged in the smithy of reality, but only reflects the thoughtless parroting of unexamined truth.

To call what happened to our son evidence of God's love flew in the face of everything I knew about love. What father delights in tormenting his children? What kind of horrible father purposely, deliberately inflicts pain on his children under the guise of teaching them a lesson? I recalled an incident I had read about years earlier of a father who set his little son on the table, then stood back a few feet and encouraged the boy to jump into his arms. When the little boy jumped, expecting father's strong arms to catch him, the father stepped back to let his suddenly terrified son crash to the floor. "This will teach you, my boy," said the cruel father, "never to trust anyone."

What warped and callous reasoning underlies such an attempt to shatter a child's trust? But if God uses the pain and the death of a child to teach his adult children a lesson, is he not really doing the same thing? How can anyone possibly be drawn closer to God or learn to love and trust him if he is the author of anguish and tragedy? For my part, I have always had difficulty trusting and feeling close to those who inflict pain of one sort or another. The constant refrain, that this was the Lord's doing, did not make my love for the Lord flourish. It was not something I could freely talk about, however. How can one ask questions of people to whom the answers are so obvious and so easy? Like Jacob, I continued my contest with God at my secret and private Jabbok.

To be sure, in Old Testament times God sometimes used sickness and death as punishments but always after giving fair warning and linking the consequence to the preceding sin. In the New Testament, on the other hand, all the miracles of Jesus with only one exception were to heal and help. How then can we still say today that God inflicts pain so we will learn to trust him? It would be so much easier to approach a warm, caring God.

I have been told that trials are designed to make people stronger and better. God sends suffering, so the reasoning goes, because he has detected spiritual or emotional weakness. The trials that he sends are intended to build up weaklings. Suffering is the high-calorie food that will build spiritual stamina and emotional strength. Suffering is like weight lifting: do enough of it and you become a giant in the eyes of the Lord and the community.

It sounds marvelous, especially to those who don't need to go through the exercises. To me it sounded hypocritical, judgmental, and phony. For one thing, I perceived in these comments a subtle rebuke, a veiled declaration that I had been weighed and found wanting, ostensibly by God, but surely by the person making the pious claims. Of course, it didn't take much in those days to make me feel less than adequate. This sort of comment, though, worked every time. The comments became an external affirmation of the doubts I already harbored within my soul. As such they became destructive rather than supportive.

Even worse than what these claims said about me is what they say about the speakers themselves. In saying that trials came to me as God's way of making me better, they were implying that they escaped because they already were better. Where I was inadequate, they measured up. Where I failed the test, they passed with flying colors. Where I still valiantly struggled, they had already arrived. These pious people did not have to worry about things like children being impaired or dying. God was on their side. How arrogant are these claims, I now think. How utterly presumptive the people who dare make them!

By now I had learned how to deal with my feelings and was able to carry out my ministry despite the growing pressures at home. Occasionally I even dared to make veiled mention in a sermon of the struggle going on in the parsonage next door. The congregation was sympathetic and in many small ways expressed their concern and support. Despite the clichés, many others found this a bewildering time, too, a time when they felt helpless to do much to diminish either our grief or their own. The more thoughtful people were forced to examine their own perception of God's involvement in this situation. Like us, they saw happiness in terms of a cure for the boy but did not know how to achieve that, anymore than we did. But in the end, we faced our burden alone, despite their love.

When vacation approached, the boy expressed a wish to see the Rockies. He had been there once before, when he was only three, but had forgotten that trip except for the pictures that reminded him of the majestic mountains. Now he talked of it again. We could hardly afford it, though the cost would be minimal if we slept in our camper. So we decided to go. It would be a refreshing change from the scene of all this frustration. We realized, though, that the escape would not really work; of necessity, the pain and frustration would come along with us wherever we went.

Why is it, I wonder now, that we went? Why is it that

people make almost sentimental journeys back to their birthplace in the few remaining months before their death? Why do people visit Disneyland or Epcot Center with a dying child, often using money they can ill afford to spend just then? Are these trips expressive of our real beliefs, symbols of a deep-rooted paganism that inwardly denies the existence of life after death while paying lip service to the doctrine that there shall be a resurrection to a life infinitely more glorious than what we now have? Why do people—why did we—cram into the last remaining months of a loved one's life activities that otherwise would never have happened? Is it a confession through our actions that this life is the only one we will have and that, if we miss pleasures here, we will never have a chance for this enjoyment again? Compared with the beauty of heaven, where we confessed our son would go, was not a trip to the Rockies similar to wallowing in a mud hole? Does dying become easier if you can carry in your mind an image of Pike's Peak?

We went, untroubled then by philosophical questions, simply to enjoy the spectacular grandeur of God's marvelous creation. Perhaps that's what we really sought all along, a confrontation with the creative power of the Almighty during this time when we experienced in our lives only the destructive influence of evil. We went, just the three of us. Our younger boy, who could neither comprehend the concept of his brother's approaching death nor enjoy the mountain vistas, stayed with his grandparents.

Almost every day we traveled a short distance, stopping frequently whenever something interesting caught our attention. I remember only occasional images of those ten days: the boy clambering to the top of huge boulders, the roaring of a mountain stream, walking in snow in the middle of the summer, jagged peaks all around us poised against a deep blue sky in which floated lazy fluffy clouds that unravelled almost as soon as they left the mountain peaks behind. I have an image of the boy eating his lunch on a roadside rock and feeding pieces of bread to a brave chipmunk who dared come within inches of his outstretched hand. I see him standing against a background of weathered sculptures in the Colorado National Monument, a boy whose life has barely begun and is already ending surrounded by rocks shaped by a million years of wind and rain. Perhaps that's what we sought, a sense of perspective that pain, however sharp, will always pass while only time remains.

The days were beautiful, the nights spectacular as we gazed at stars infinitely more bright and numerous than ever we saw at home. While the twinkling lights of passing planes reminded us that we lived in an inhabited world, we felt part of an ever-expanding universe of which even the farthest fringes were nevertheless held firmly by the hands of God. Perhaps that is what we needed, this reminder that, if he can keep track of billions of planets, God is big enough to remember one dying little boy and his family.

But also at night—always at night—there were the cries of pain. During the day, the constantly changing vistas helped the boy suppress an awareness of his pain. At night, however, even after he slept, there was only the sharp throbbing for which the pills we gave him brought little relief. Without fail each night we were torn back from the splendor of heaven to the torment of this private hell inseparably linked to us wherever we went. But for our pain there were no pills. And the beauty of the days could never quite erase the terrors of the nights.

That summer, men walked on the moon for the first time ever. Though we, too, marveled at this "giant step" of which mankind was capable, the achievement paled beside the wistful question: why, when men could snare the moon and make it merely a neighborhood—why was there no cure for cancer? Who cares about footprints in moon dust when you walk beside someone whose tiny prints will soon be gone forever?

On Sunday, while those men explored the moon, we worshiped beneath the gleaming spires of the Air Force Academy Chapel. The chaplain spoke eloquently about the scientific breakthrough brought into every living room via television. He went much beyond that, however, when he began to speak on words from John: "How great is the love the Father has lavished on us, that we should be called children of God! And that is what we are! . . . Dear friends, now we are children of God, and what we will be has not yet been made known. But we know that when he appears, we shall be like him, for we shall see him as he is" (1 John 3:1, 2).

As he spoke, my eyes stayed glued to the delicately sculpted floating cross. I thought of Christ, his life and healing touch, his death on Calvary. And all along, the words were said again, "The greatest miracle today is still that God makes us his children, in love, through Christ, forever!" Men walking on a dusty moon can never equal what one Man did that Friday long ago as he walked a dusty road to death. The impact of moon flights on our lives is passing. Atonement gives us an inheritance that never fades away.

Just the same, though we were children of the Almighty, the boy's pains got worse. Reluctantly, we went home earlier than planned, in many ways inspired and yet worn out more than when we had left home.

The boy was content. For him it had been a great vacation. When he talked of where to go next year, we fell silent.

eight ❧

In September, the boy celebrated his eighth birthday and entered third grade. Sending him to school was an act of faith, an investment in a future that we still—though faintly—hoped would be bright with the joy of healing. Keeping him home would have been a surrender to defeat and unacceptable despair. School attendance was also a testimony to our conviction—a conviction sometimes submerged in despair—that God expects all his children to develop their abilities to the fullest potential, using each day well regardless of what tomorrow may bring. The boy was well enough to enjoy school and benefit from its programs. It filled his time and gave him a sense of purpose.

Although he was still growing slightly, his weight no longer kept pace. It peaked at fifty-one pounds. During one hospital visit, the doctor tried to reduce our concern by joking that the boy was almost square. The numbers for his height and weight were nearly identical, though even those numbers underscored that the cancer was winning. He did not stay "square" long. He gradually became thinner.

I remember the subtle, slow, persistent progress of the disease. Like an invisible but voracious snake making up for the time lost during the period of remission it swallowed him up, draining away the luster of his complexion, hollowing out his cheeks, attacking his muscles and nerves.

It began with the legs. He had always been filled with boundless energy and great courage. He loved to run, he played hard, he rode his old bike with reckless abandon, he climbed trees with the daring and agility of a squirrel. Gradually, relentlessly all that changed. With the passing of time, walking became more difficult, running impossible, climbing trees out of the question. Though he still spent every possible moment outdoors, an unhealthy pallor replaced the deep tan burned into his skin by the summer sun. His face thinned ever so slightly and the constant pain etched lines beside his mouth. Dark shadows formed around his eyes. The changes were barely perceptible to others, but to us alarming as we scanned him each day for some new sign of decline.

The question of whether to tell him that he was dying suddenly became academic. He came home from school one afternoon, walked into the kitchen where his mother was beginning to prepare dinner, and said, "Jimmy says that I'm going to die pretty soon." Then, without waiting for a reply, he skipped out the door with a rare burst of energy to play outside.

I don't recall just what we said to him. That evening, however, when the supper dishes were cleared away, we explained to him what was happening in his body. We talked about tumors and malignancies. We explained what the radiation treatments and the chemotherapy had tried to accomplish, and how it had all failed. We explained what the doctors thought would happen to him next. We affirmed that Jimmy had been right. Yes, he would soon die. We told him how much we loved him, how desperately we wanted to keep him with us and for that reason had tried all those treatments. We shared with him how afraid we had been for almost two years now, how we had not told him about the possibility of dying because we did not want him to be afraid. Our silence had not been a matter of dishonesty but of love, of wanting to shelter him as long as possible from the cruel reality he faced.

Even after all these years I cannot quite comprehend how we managed to tell our son so calmly about his impending death and about the suffering that could possibly precede it. Other parents have the privilege of discussing what their children will become when they grow up. They can afford to chuckle over the fantasies of their little ones who want to be firefighters or astronauts or doctors or presidents because they know that, as time goes on, the children will outgrow the fantasies. For us, every word we said that dreadful night tore to shreds whatever remnants of tattered hope still remained. Our reality was that of an eight-year-old who had very likely just celebrated his last birthday and would never see another. Our task was to prepare our son for the process of dying, to alleviate his fears, to kindle hope in his heart.

We had to do all that while our own fears grew and while our last hope evaporated and while no one helped prepare us for the loss that would come. We did not want to fail the boy. Both my wife and I wanted him to feel loved and safe to the very end. And so we poured all our energies into him while neglecting ourselves and each other. "No man is an island," wrote John Donne, "any man's death diminishes me." How much more does the death diminish parents when the man is not yet a man but only a little boy, *their* boy, and no sacrifice, however great, can turn back the inevitable?

For his part, the boy was rather silent. He asked few questions, and I remember none of them. What is it like, to be eight years old and be told that you will soon die? What does an eight-year-old know of death? I recalled an episode during the Second World War—when I happened to be eight years old. One day, a friend and I were hunted by four German soldiers because we foolishly had taunted them with an anti-Nazi song. The terror we then felt is still vividly impressed upon my mind, along with the relief when at last we managed to outwit and escape them because we knew the area like we knew our back pockets. Did the cancer terrify the boy the way those four tall soldiers with guns had terrified me? He had never been to a funeral, never seen a dead person, though he had heard of those in the congregation who died and he was aware that some people suddenly no longer came to church. Not one of them had been young, however.

We talked about heaven that night and about Jesus who would be waiting for him there. But what is heaven? What comfort is it to go there when you have no inkling of what heaven is all about and when you have never met Jesus but only know about him from what others say? How utterly frightening the future must be when you're only eight years old and you have just learned that you must leave your family against your will, to go somewhere all alone while your mom and dad and little brother cannot come along. We tried to show the boy our love and assured him how much we would miss him. But they now seem so futile, all those words, and I wonder whether anything we said really helped.

In his poem "Home Burial," Robert Frost has written,

> The nearest friends can go
> with anyone to death, comes so far short.
> They might as well not try to go at all.
> No, from the time when one is sick to death
> one is alone, and he dies more alone.

One hears of people with cancer or some other terminal disease being shunned by those whom they believed to be friends. Our boy was never shunned; nevertheless, the contemplation of death began to move him gently into a world of his own, a world where we could not follow. We could still look forward to a future for ourselves. We could make plans for next year and for five years down the road. He could do none of that, while knowing that whatever plans we spun could not include him anymore. Not that we purposely excluded him, far from it. So often, though, when we talked about an event like Christmas or "next summer," we suddenly realized that by then the boy would almost surely not be with us anymore.

And now he knew it, too.

Time passed with agonizing reluctance. Always there was that pain, that excruciating pain that tormented the boy at night and progressively by day as well. From time to time he asked questions about death and the process of dying, about heaven and whether anyone there would know him. It was an indication that in the privacy of his soul he was continually processing all that shocking information we had shared with him, sorting out what he could understand from what was yet incomprehensible.

Thanksgiving came and with it my challenge to prepare a sermon befitting the day. I looked at the injunction given so long ago by the apostle Paul to the Thessalonians: "Be joyful always; pray continually; give thanks in all circumstances, for this is God's will for you in Christ Jesus" (1 Thessalonians 5:16–18). I recalled a line from one of Elizabeth Barrett Browning's poems: "Some people always sigh in thanking God." Somehow I managed to get ready, but my struggle was evident.

"Try once," I said to my congregation, "to give thanks without sighing when you take a hard look at the circumstances in which you live. How do you sincerely give thanks without sighing for a crop that was not exactly bad, nor very good? How do you give thanks without sighing for a job that is steady but pays you barely enough to support your family? How do you give thanks without sighing for your family when the relationship between family members is strained almost to the breaking point? How do you give thanks without sighing if a loved one is taken from you? How do you give thanks without sighing when you are confronted by a disease that has no cure and will shortly run its course? Yes, indeed, talk is cheap, but try once to give sincere thanks under those circumstances."

Yet this is what God asks of us. This is his will for us in Christ Jesus that somehow, despite our disappointment and pain, we look for bright spots in the dark periods of our lives. I was grateful that Paul did not say we need to give thanks *for* all circumstances, but only *in* all circumstances. That is challenge enough. To give thanks *for* cancer was more than I could manage then or now.

My Christmas message a month later also reflected the situation at home. On the basis of Luke 2:10 and 19, I explained how the birth of Mary's first child was for her at once great joy and great apprehension. I observed that "Jesus was born in a place where they did not really belong, a place where Mary could not call one single thing her own. And the point of it all was that even Jesus did not really belong just to her. He belonged to the world, to the millions of people who pray that God will save them from their sins and their sicknesses. Other mothers can make plans for their children, but not Mary. Other mothers and fathers can dream about the day when the child will be grown, get married, have children of his own. But not Mary. . . . A mother's instinct is so very strong. A mother doesn't want to give up her child. It is hard when God comes to ask for your child because he has something else in mind for that child, something different from what you have in mind."

Talking about the coming of the Savior, that Christmas, did little to minimize the pain we felt about the going away of our son. Knowing about the one did not help much in dealing with the other.

We celebrated Christmas as usual, with gifts for all, including the boy. He had talked much about wanting a new bike. When he received his first one three years earlier, it was a used one. He wanted a new one then but accepted a used bike after we persuaded him that it would be better to learn on an old one. By now, hard use had taken its toll on the old bike and almost every day I repaired one thing or another that no longer worked or was broken. We had added the promise that we would buy a new bike when he reached third grade and really knew how to handle one. Little did we know, when we made that promise, what would happen during those next three years. The boy had not forgotten the agreement, however, and regularly reminded us that now it was our turn to keep the bargain. Lately, to our pain, the old bike had seen little use and not merely because it was now winter. The boy had increasing difficulty moving the pedals round, especially going uphill. Whenever he mentioned the new bike, we stalled or changed the subject. There was no bike for Christmas, either, to the boy's disappointment. We talked about it, reluctantly, and explained why. There was no point anymore, we said, in buying a bike. He could not ride it now because of the cold and snow but, more importantly, his muscles no longer functioned well. The boy agreed, though barely convinced it really had to be this way.

It was a way of making the process of dying more real, all this talk of riding a bike. This is what dying is all about. It is being unable to climb trees anymore, having difficulty walking, being in almost constant pain, not getting a new bike for Christmas because you won't live long enough to use it.

The boy was angry at times—at us for not keeping our word and not giving him the bike; sometimes at God for giving him so much pain and now making him die. He argued and questioned.

"Why do I have to die now?"

My answers were less than convincing. I didn't know either. I was still wrestling with the "why" of all of this. I could not bring myself to tell the boy that his illness and pain were gifts from God, signs of God's love. For one thing, I did not believe it myself. For another, I feared that any talk that linked his pain with God's love would only make him more rebellious and angry.

He knew a great deal about God and Jesus. From his kindergarten days he had attended a Christian day school where children heard Bible stories each day and were taught to pray. He had gone to Sunday school. At home we prayed before and after each meal, and read from the Bible as a sort of spiritual dessert. He had never questioned anything that he learned about God. From all appearances, God and Jesus were real to him. He loved them and was convinced they loved him. Now was the time for him to evaluate spiritual truths. Now he needed to sort through all that information he had absorbed over the years and, hopefully, discover the valuable nuggets he needed to endure in the coming months. Though he was only eight, he had to do it for himself. We could be there to help and support, but we could not make him believe. He himself had to go through the process that would make his childlike faith grow to its highest spiritual maturity.

It didn't help to tell the story of Job and explain that it was not really God but Satan who so horribly tortured innocent, righteous Job and who was doubtlessly behind this cancer. As the boy observed one day, in his incisive

92

way, "If God simply sits back and allows Satan to do this to me, it's still his fault, isn't it? He could tell Satan to stop, can't he?"

Nor did it help much, not yet, to talk of the healing miracles of Jesus and how they showed that God does not really want people to be sick and suffer but wants them healthy and whole. "Then why doesn't Jesus make me better? I've asked him, but I'm still sick."

We kept visiting the hospital all through that winter, but the visits brought no encouragement. Although X-rays and bloods tests barely confirmed the presence of cancer, visual observation made the ravages of the disease clear enough. There was no more reason to hope. The boy would not get better.

Visits to the pharmacy also became more frequent. When regular medication no longer brought any relief from the pain, the boy graduated to narcotics. At first, the dosages were rigidly prescribed and adhered to. It soon became evident he needed more codeine, more frequently. Even that brought only limited relief. Those times we needed to go away for an evening and leave him with a sitter, ordinarily something he thoroughly enjoyed, the boy went into a near-panic that the sitter would possibly refuse to give him pain pills when he needed them. While he was present we told her to give them whenever the boy asked for them. It was hardly sufficient. At last we simply left the bottle where the boy could reach it, always giving a time before which he could not have a pill. He handled the responsibility well and one problem was solved. The question surfaced of side effects and possible drug dependency but was quickly laid to rest when the doctor remarked laconically, "Under the circumstances there's little point in worrying about that."

Despite his now-constant and severe pain, the boy continued to attend school. As winter progressed, the tumor made it increasingly difficult for him to sit at the desk; consequently, he spent much of the school day standing up. Eventually, he only went mornings. He always walked to and from school, a short distance that ordinarily took only a minute or two. Only the church stood between the parsonage and school. I recall seeing him come home from school at noon, those very last days he still attended. With difficulty but stubborn determination he'd walk the short distance from school to the church steps. There he'd sit down for a while to rest while I watched from my upstairs study window. At times I'd see him wipe tears from his eyes as he silently cried. After a while he'd struggle to his feet and laboriously walk the rest of the way home. I offered to pick him up at school, but he refused. Several times we suggested it was time to stay home for good.

"No way. I can easily make it. I won't quit."

On an early spring day, he asked me to bring up his bike from the basement where it had been stored for the winter. I demurred on the grounds that he was out of practice, that it would hurt too much, that he might fall and injure himself. My words fell on deaf ears. He was determined, unshakable. It was almost as though he had to prove to himself that all the predictions were wrong, that he would live instead of die, that he was stronger than this tumor in his back.

"But I want to ride the bike, Dad. Please!"

How does one refuse a dying boy? I brought up the bike and helped him get on. He could still ride though with visible effort and obvious pain. With me running beside him, he peddled to the parking lot between the church and school. Just then, school was being dismissed. The children and some parents saw him ride and cheered, then they left and after a few minutes we went back home. The boy sprawled on the floor, delighted but totally exhausted.

94

That evening, a long-scheduled school program was held. We all went. Just before the closing prayer, the president of the school board called our son to the front. He looked at me, his face reflecting surprise and questions. I didn't know either what was happening but urged him to go forward. As the boy reached the front, someone wheeled in a brand-new, shiny green bike with a banana seat and tall, chrome backbar. It was the exact model the boy had always talked about, apparently not only to us. The board president mentioned how they had seen the boy ride that afternoon, how impressed they were with his determination, and how some of the students had decided on the spur of the moment that he should have the new bike he had so long dreamed about. And should have it right now. Somehow they came up with the money in only a few hours. Somehow they found the right bike. There it was, the best possible symbol of love and encouragement anyone could have devised.

Both my wife and I had difficulty controlling our emotions. Unbidden tears came to our eyes. The boy was speechless, unable to believe his eyes, his face radiating unfeigned joy. Though we had trained him long ago to be polite, this time it never occurred to him to say "thank you." He simply looked back and forth from the bike to the president, overcome by a reality that, for once, was so incredibly good to him.

As soon as the program was finished and the parking lot empty he climbed on his new bike and rode around in the dark for just a few minutes. Then, when we got home, the new bike was parked in the family room where no bike had ever stood before. The boy went to bed where sleep came with difficulty for him, as it did for us much later.

After this day of surprises, however, he rode his bike only two more times, less than a mile altogether and both times with my help.

95

nine &

Only a few weeks after receiving his new bike, the boy's continual sharp pain teamed up with muscular weakness to make standing and walking nearly impossible. By now his left leg was much thinner than the other; both refused to work any longer. During checkups the sensory test conducted with the sharp and dull ends of a pin revealed that he no longer had any feeling in the feet and only limited feeling in the upper leg and thighs. Along with the muscles, the nervous system was deteriorating as a result of the incessant pressure of the ever-growing tumor. That invisible, irresistible monster snake was still there, devouring our precious son before our eyes. We could do nothing about it.

The end of the school year was in sight. Though he wanted to stay in school to finish the third grade, the boy had to admit that it was no longer possible. He still rejected my offer to bring him and pick him up, not giving a reason but leaving little doubt that this was too humiliating for him. So he stayed home, closing the door on that important part of his life that he would never again enter. More than anything, this brought home to all of us the reality that his illness was irreversible and accelerating. In the process, he lost almost all contacts with his classmates. He allowed only a few of his close friends to come into the house to play with him on occasion. He was too ashamed of his condition and simply refused to see people who were not part of that select inner group with whom he felt comfortable. For him, the experience of dying—that sad, melancholy process of severing ties with everything on earth—had now begun.

We found a child-sized wheelchair and, over the boy's protests, brought it home. It enabled him to attend church on Sunday morning or go with us on shopping trips. It also made it easier to take him for his regular checkups at the hospital. The boy tried to ignore the stares of children and adults by pretending interest in other things. Still, his pain and embarrassment were obvious. He, who had been so active and exuberantly healthy, now was an invalid.

As parents, we felt a different pain. Here we were, walking through the mall with two children, one in a wheelchair and the other obviously retarded, and pretending all was normal when in reality we wished there was some hole where we could hide till this storm of anguish had passed. In blessed ignorance, our retarded son was the only one for whom nothing was out of the ordinary.

The wheelchair had one totally unexpected consequence. All at once, we became aware of what life is like for a person confined to a chair. We discovered how uneven the sidewalk was between the parsonage and the church. Those steps into the house and into almost every other building that in the past had simply been there as part of the architecture now loomed large. Before, they had been, at most, nuisances. Now, they were major obstacles. I could see how for many people in wheelchairs, steps, narrow doors, and even thresholds are barricades that keep them from attending events where our presence is simply taken for granted. I became adept at lugging that chair, with my son in it, up stairways or letting it down again gently, one step at a time, trying to minimize bouncing as much as possible to avoid unnecessary pain. We were lucky; his weight was so slight now that the chair hardly represented a burden. But what, I thought, is it like for an adult who is barred from, say, attending church because of those seven steps at the entrance to the sanctuary? How painfully humiliating, to be prevented from going where you so badly want to go because you're in a chair and because no one has yet thought about putting in a ramp or a lift! This, at least, our son did not face. He could go wherever I could pull him.

At home, however, the boy refused to use the chair. It was bad enough he needed it in public. In the privacy of home he preferred to crawl over the floor even though this aggravated his pain. I still see him struggle to get to the bathroom, a laborious trip that asserted his resolution that as long as he could do something for himself no one would do it for him.

One day he read in the paper that someone was selling a miniature poodle. He had often talked about having a pet but for various reasons we had never given him one. In the past he had always accepted our refusals with good grace, just as he was obedient in everything else. But now it was different. He turned on the pressure for this dog.

"But Dad, it's a good dog—it says so right here. And he's purebred. He comes with papers."

I tried to sidetrack him with a sick joke. "Those papers are probably because he's not housebroken. He'll go all over the place, and the house will smell like a barnyard."

"Dad, you're being silly. Can I have him?"

My attempt to use money as an excuse also backfired. Looking back to it, it was hardly fair for me to bring up this topic. The only reason money was scarce at our house was because of the boy's enormous medical bills. Now I used it, thoughtlessly, against him. "What do you think a dog like that will cost? Purebred animals are special and they're expensive. We don't have money for a dog."

"That's no problem, Dad. I've got lots of money. Think of all the money people have given me when I was in the hospital. Let's call and find out how much the dog costs. And I'll pay for him."

Triumph for him and defeat for me. The boy and his mother went to see the dog and before long came home with him. Sparky was a beautiful little dog, almost all white, with just a hint of rust over his spine and at the tip of his constantly wagging tail. He was a friendly animal, a curly bundle of energy that set the house topsy-turvy until we were all used to each other. The boy was thrilled with having his very own pet. His little brother was even more taken with Sparky and played with him constantly. When Sparky wanted peace he came to my study and slept curled up against my feet. Before long, we all loved the little dog and wondered why we had waited so long to adopt a pet.

To our surprise, less than a month passed when the boy began to talk about selling the dog. There were two reasons. Now that he spent increasing amounts of time in bed, the dog did not pay so much attention to him anymore but more to his brother. Since it was his dog, paid for with his own money, that hardly seemed fair. The other reason was that, whenever he was in bed and called Sparky, the dog jumped on the bed. The jarring of the mattress caused the pain in his leg and back to flare up. He did not dare call the dog. He did not dare leave Sparky alone for fear he would lose the dog completely. Hence this unexpected desire to sell him.

We did not want to give up the dog, however, especially because our second son was so enamored with his new playmate. The dog had almost become a substitute for the older brother who rarely played with him anymore. I offered to buy the dog from the boy. That way he would have his money back, the dog would be my dog instead of his, and he would not have to worry anymore about losing control of the dog yet could still play with him whenever he wanted. It seemed like a fair deal to all concerned, and the boy accepted. He was not satisfied for long, however. Giving up the dog, while the dog was still around, was too painful for him. He became a little envious of his brother who spent so much time with Sparky. One day the boy surprised me.

"Dad, I want to buy Sparky back from you."

"That's fine with me, but why would you want to do that? You can do anything with Sparky now. You don't need to buy him for that."

"Well, it's this way. If you'll sell him back to me, I can sell him to somebody outside of this house. Then I don't have to see him anymore."

I laughed at the ingenious scheme without quite understanding then the motives behind it. I told the boy that we were all attached to the little dog, especially his brother, and that it would not be fair to sell him. Reluctantly, the boy closed the subject and made the best of the situation. Sparky stayed.

Early that spring, my wife learned she was pregnant, news that stirred up mixed emotions. We feared the possibility that perhaps this new baby would be born handicapped like the previous child. We also dreaded the prospect of having one little boy who was so very slow and needed help with almost everything, another who was becoming increasingly more dependent as the cancer took its toll, and then a little baby besides. How would we possibly cope? *God, why are you doing this to us? Why now?* Too many things were happening to us, too rapidly. We had difficulty coping with all of it, even more difficulty seeing God's hand in this pregnancy. What we needed was less responsibility, not more.

The boy, however, was delighted. A new baby in the house? Here, in our house? Because of our preoccupation with his illness, sex education had been virtually ignored. Suddenly he was filled with a million questions. He wanted to know all about babies, where they come from, why they grow inside the mother, how they got there. Another question occurred to him.

"How is the baby going to get out of there?"

We answered his questions truthfully. He could hardly wait for the day the baby would arrive. We had not the heart to tell him that he might not live to see it. That thought never even occurred to him as he spun his dreams about the new baby brother or sister who was growing inside his mother. He simply decided that he would be there when the day came and that was that. After having to give up so much already, he suddenly had something to live for again. He had hope again, and it was bright.

Increasingly he began to miss church as the periods became shorter that he could endure sitting in his wheelchair. We began the routine of having sitters come in during the morning service so my wife could at least attend once each Sunday. Girls and women in the congregation willingly offered their services, though the boy was selective about who could and who could not stay with him. Being absent from church increased his interest in what happened there. When I came home after the service, he asked me what I had preached about. Sometimes he would ask questions. At times he even asked me to read my sermon notes to him so he would hear almost the whole sermon all over again. We began to realize this was an unusual eight-year-old. While physically his condition deteriorated with each passing day, he grew spiritually and became more and more interested in the things of the Lord.

One Sunday, in a sermon on life after death, I quoted

Luke 20:36, "They can no longer die; for they are like the angels. They are God's children, since they are children of the resurrection." When I retold the sermon at home for the boy's benefit, his eyes lit up when he heard this text. He thought for a while, then interrupted me, "Aren't those beautiful names that Jesus used, Dad? 'Children of God' and 'children of the resurrection.' And to think I'm going there!"

A few days later he was still thinking about it. The subject of heaven came up again at the supper table. For devotions afterward I read parts of Revelation 21 and 22, that enticingly beautiful picture of the new heaven and new earth that the Apostle John describes in such glowing terms. The boy never liked apples very much. When he heard that in the new Jerusalem fruit trees grow beside the River of Life, bearing a different fruit every month, he responded in his dry way, "I guess, when I get there, I'll even like apples."

We laughed, just as we still managed to laugh a lot even in those days. Yet just below the surface of the laughter was that lingering pain in our hearts over that irresistibly coming separation when the boy would go to be with the Lord and we would stay behind. It was no longer a source of agonizing struggle. We no longer prayed for healing. We no longer had any hope for that whatever nor did we expect any miracles. Long since, the awareness had settled in our hearts that God had no intention of hearing either our prayers or those of our friends. We had no idea what God had in mind with all this. But at least we now had the ability to accept the inevitable reality and know that God was at work even in this illness.

ten 〜

That last summer we took no vacation, except for a three-day stay in a cabin at a lake not far from the hospital where we needed to go once again for a checkup. The doctors spoke of a new medication that might possibly slow the progress of the disease though they did not believe it would diminish the pain. We decided not to use the medication. The boy would die; why prolong his agony? And ours?

Satan's bold and arrogant words to God came to mind: "Skin for skin . . . A man will give all he has for his own life. But stretch out your hand and touch his flesh and bones, and he will surely curse you to your face" (Job 2:4–5).

No, we would not give everything for the life of our son, nor for our own, if we had been sick ourselves. We made the decision then that all subsequent medical treatment would have one single-minded goal: to alleviate the boy's pain and make his last days as comfortable as possible. The quality of his life would take precedence over the quantity remaining. We also decided that, should his condition deteriorate to the point of needing life-support systems or other so-called "heroic" measures, the boy would not get them. We would not allow him to be hooked to some machine that could breathe for him. Not for him an artificially prolonged life that benefited neither him nor anyone else. No, now that we had reconciled ourselves to his coming death, we prayed he would be alert till the end—and then go quickly.

Having made this momentous decision we rested as best we could at the lake. We sprawled on the sun-drenched beach with both our boys and watched as boats pulled graceful waterskiers in their wake. The boy was envious, wishing he could still learn something like that, yet painfully aware the time for new skills was forever past. That night we floated across the lake on an excursion boat. Returning to shore, the boat was attacked by several canoes filled with obviously hostile "Indians" whose whooping war cries and frightening war paint boded little good. They were boy scouts from a nearby camp, and the raid prearranged. Though some managed to clamber on board where they stayed temporarily, they were eventually beaten off and left astern hanging bedraggled onto their capsized canoes. The boy loved it, though again it was something he would never do himself.

My wife was now visibly pregnant, and the boy kept close tabs on those developments. He was allowed to feel her stomach and marveled at the miraculous way in which God creates a new person. It was a period of discovery for him, as it was for us.

Gradually his pain became more severe. During the day he needed his medication with increasing frequency. We gave it without questioning his need; the doctor refilled prescriptions without demurring. During the night his sleep was interrupted as he awoke at regular intervals to ask for a pill. In between, he frequently cried out during his sleep. We took turns getting up to rub his back and legs or, since a massage rarely helped anymore, just sit with him to hold his hand and talk whenever he was awake. The more my wife needed rest for herself and the developing baby, the more these nocturnal duties fell on me.

I recall the frustration of those endless nights when, once awakened, I could never go back to sleep. How I wished for some miracle that would take the pain away, that would allow the boy to sleep peacefully through even one night. During those hours of lingering darkness, despair threatened to creep over me time and again. Burdensome as the days may have been, the nights were so much worse. There is something about darkness that has the power to terrify the human soul. Darkness creates an infinite loneliness because it hides all familiar landmarks and faces; all the ghosts and demons that lurk in the subconscious swarm like bats to the surface, unnoticed and unchecked until they are already flying loose. During the night, songs turn to sobs in one's throat and prayers bounce aimlessly off the wall. God should have been there during those interminable hours of darkness, and sometimes he was. Most frequently, however, the screams of the boy drowned out any thoughts of God.

Oh, how I dreaded those nights and longed for morning. As I sat there beside the bed, I remembered reading about a mother who killed her incurably ill child. She called it an act of love, done out of the desire to spare her suffering child further pain. At the time I wondered how any parent could resort to such a grotesque act. Now, as the minutes ticked away in the darkness, I knew how she could do it and why. I no longer blamed her but almost envied her desperate courage and devotion. There were moments when I too was tempted. I thought about how simple it would be to give the boy a few extra pills and then press a pillow over his face. In just a few minutes all his suffering would be over, and he would float out of this agonizing darkness into the dazzling brilliance of God's presence where all things would be made new and he would never again shed a tear. Someone who has not lived with a dying loved one will never be able to understand this desperate

107

urge to end the struggle and may even be shocked that a Christian father, a minister no less, could entertain such thoughts, could think of murder while calling it love. But such was the reality some of those agonizing nights.

It would have been so easy to act as that mother acted, yet I never translated the secret fantasy into reality. I hesitated not because of fear of prosecution. Any punishment seemed a small price to pay as long as my son no longer suffered. Besides, I was not so certain there would be any punishment. Nor was it fear of God or the conviction I have always held that the taking of a life, any life at any stage of its existence, is morally wrong. God would understand, I reasoned, and God would forgive. No, what really held me back was the nagging fear that in some split-second of final awareness my son might know what I was doing and would question my love. And so I simply sat holding his hands, those nights when the boy cried out in his agony, and gradually changed my prayer from "God take the pain away" to "God, take the boy away. Quickly!"

The summer had a few other highlights. A couple in our church invited us to spend a day at their cottage at a nearby lake. That afternoon we sped over the lake in their powerboat. Even the boy mustered up enough strength to sit behind the wheel a short time and steer. Later, when the boy was back in another seat and leaned over the edge to trail his hands through the swiftly moving water, the boat's owner flinched uncomfortably at the sight of that disfiguring bulge on my son's back. He whispered to me, "So that's what you contend with all the time. It's all so tragic. How do you cope?"

One sunny day, a week or so later, I borrowed someone's dune buggy—a converted Volkswagen—and lifted my son into the seat next to me. For an hour we drove around the area in an exhilarating high-speed ride. Though an occasional sharp bump in the road made him wince with pain, the boy could hardly get enough of the feel of the wind in his face and the thrill of speed. When we returned home, he was reluctant to leave this fun vehicle.

Also that summer, the boy and I accompanied some friends on a leisurely evening boat ride down a nearby river. As we floated beneath the arch formed by overhanging trees we explored the eroding banks unsuccessfully for signs that Indians had once been there. Mosquitoes swarmed around us whenever the breeze slackened. It was a relaxing, healing trip. After all these years I can still visualize the boy perched on pillows in the stern, against the backdrop of the tree-linked banks, the setting sun shining on his happy face.

Incredibly, the boy celebrated yet another birthday, his ninth. He had now lived six times longer than the six months initially predicted. His weight continued to drop as he increasingly struggled with food that no longer appealed to him. I could easily pick him up to carry him up the stairs to his bedroom at night and down again in the morning. His legs were now little more than cruelly twisted sticks, no longer capable of carrying any weight at all. His arms, though they still functioned, were fast becoming equally skinny. Only the tumor on his back had not diminished. Larger than ever, it bulged under that long scar and the surrounding tissue that had turned a dark tan from the many doses of radiation.

By now he had difficulty sitting in his chair for more than a few minutes. He rarely left the house anymore but spent most of the day lying on a foam mattress on the floor where he could watch television. Sparky, the little poodle, often rested right beside him. His road racing set was laid out in a twisting course on the family-room floor. He hardly ever·played with it anymore since he could no longer move to put cars back on the track once they missed a curve and sailed off.

We had a birthday party, attended by the relatives who lived nearby. Somehow it turned into a fun event with some games and much laughter. The boy lay on his mattress in the middle of the circle and enjoyed the attention. Though we all knew that there could not possibly ever be another party for him, it did not really seem to matter anymore. Instead of anxiously hoping for a miracle because we so desperately wanted to keep the boy with us, we now treasured each day as a unique and precious gift, despite the pain that still spoiled most nights.

Again the cards came. Again with money in most of them. The well-wishers were as stumped as we were about knowing what presents to buy for a boy who already had a closet filled with toys but no strength to play with them. Money was the easy way out. The boy simply counted the dollars and told us to put them into his savings account. Because the old television set almost continually produced a distorted, rolling picture, we decided to buy a new set and call it a birthday present. It was not really in the budget but by now we were so far in debt that it seemed to make little difference whether we spent a bit more, this time for fun.

Besides being emotionally draining, this illness became a major financial burden. Our insurance covered a large part of the hospital, doctor, and pharmacy bills but by no means all of it. There were all those other related costs, however, like the frequent trips to the hospital for checkups, the long periods where we needed to stay in an expensive guest home or motel, the many meals we ate in restaurants. These were the little financial dribbles that, despite our frugality, combined into a torrent for which there was no reimbursement. While our church provided some assistance, we ended up borrowing amounts that we didn't know when or how to repay. We became aware of the heartless statement of one man that, if we could not afford this kind of medical care for our child, we should simply let him die. Others said that, if money could cure, the money would come. Somehow, however, the money never came to cover these incidental expenses. Because of my early childhood experience of living with poverty these debts bothered me, though I could do nothing about them now.

Then the boy gave me a new perspective. One day, when the mail brought several medical bills that I could not possibly pay, I voiced my frustration over having a job that paid relatively little, over having no money to pay these bills and not knowing how we would ever get them paid. "If only we weren't so confoundedly poor, this whole business would be more bearable."

He overheard. If he took the remark personally or took it to mean I resented his illness or him, he gave no indication of that. With a gentle rebuke, he became my teacher and put me to shame. "Don't say we're poor, Dad! Christians are never poor. When you've got faith, you're rich. You told me so yourself when you read from the Bible, 'Seek first the kingdom of God and God will give you everything else.'"

That was not quite how the text went, but I got the point. The words of Jesus came to mind and somehow they seemed directly spoken to me: "Unless you change and become like little children, you will never enter the kingdom of heaven" (Matthew 18:3). I had a long way to go.

About this time, a checkup revealed that the cancer had at last spread beyond his back. There now were tumors in the boy's lungs. At the hospital the doctors suggested a six-week course of chemotherapy that, while not expected to check the growth of these new tumors, would lessen the pain. So the boy and I began the once-a-week trip to and from the hospital. By leaving early in the morning and

111

returning late in the evening, and with efficient scheduling at the hospital, we could do it all in one day. The boy lay in the back of the car where I had filled in the space between the seats and covered it with foam pillows. It was a comfortable bed where he rested contentedly. Because his mother was only a few weeks from delivery, she stayed home while the two of us treasured this time together.

He was still full of questions. While on occasion he expressed fear over the prospect of dying, a fear that I tried to remove by talking about the beauty of heaven and the love he would experience there, he became more and more excited at the prospect of seeing Jesus. I recall some of his surprising remarks, reflecting that he had become a philosopher, wise far beyond his nine years. "Dad, when I was a kid, I never realized that kids can die too."

I suppressed the urge to ask him what he thought he was now. Somehow, age seemed unimportant. Unnatural though it may be for a child to die before his father, this little boy had surpassed me and was far closer to dying than I. And far more ready. When was it, I wondered, that my son left behind his childhood to reach this amazing maturity?

He was a theologian, drawing on what he had learned at home, in church and Sunday School, and now from our discussions. We talked about heaven, about whether we shall recognize people there, how it is possible for us to know those who lived centuries ago, whether it is possible for those there to remember things and people here or see what is happening. I tried to picture heaven in human terms.

"Think about heaven this way. The moment you get there, you will see Jesus and God. You will recognize them immediately and they will know you. You will be part of one big family where you will be loved more than we ever loved you. When you walk along the streets of heaven you'll meet the Apostle Peter on the street, and you'll say, 'Good morning, Peter,' and he will know your name and talk back to you. Except that everyone will have a new name, not the old ones from down here, but special ones that God will give you. And no, I don't think you'll ever miss us, though we'll miss you a great deal."

We talked about Jesus, how he was sent to die for our sins, how he rose from the dead and now is in heaven. I summarized the promises of John 14 for him where Jesus urged his disciples not to be troubled but to believe in God and in Jesus who would go to heaven to prepare a place for them in his Father's mansions. The boy reflected for a while, then remarked, "Isn't that amazing that Jesus is preparing a place for *me* in his Father's house? He really loves me. And I love him. I can't wait to see him!"

Only nine years old. He would never have a chance to make a public commitment to the Lord Jesus Christ before a fellowship of Christians. He would never taste here the bread and wine of the Lord's Supper. There was not a shred of doubt in my mind, however, that before many weeks had passed he would celebrate communion with Jesus and all the saints in glory.

One of the men of the church offered to come along with us on one of the trips. I asked the boy what he thought and he said it would be fine with him. We accepted the offer and the man came along. We quickly regretted our decision. While we had a good time, it was not the same. The boy thought so too. The moment we reached home that night, he said, "Let's not ever take anyone along with us again, Dad. It's no fun because we can't talk together when there's somebody else. All you do is talk about grownup stuff."

We made the remaining trips alone. At the hospital, the boy still showed his bravery as he stoically endured being poked until the nurse found a suitable vein, then laid patiently on the bed while the liquids dripped into his veins. Occasionally a nurse commented on his unbelievable stamina and courage. Gaunt and emaciated though he had become, he was an inspiration to those whom he met.

Then the baby came. Much of the motivation behind the boy's determination to live was that he wanted to see the new baby. He became increasingly concerned over the birth process. So intimately acquainted now with excruciating pain himself, he worried about how all of this would hurt his Mom. For weeks, his mother's coming pains loomed larger than his own.

When the time came for my wife to go to the hospital, one night just after I came home from a late meeting of the church board, a neighbor who had often sat with the children came to our home. Since the boy was in his bed upstairs, I called another neighbor and asked him to carry the boy downstairs come morning if I was not home again. We told the boy we were leaving. He unsuccessfully tried to mask his fear and panic.

Morning came, but the labor pains had stopped. The obstetrician who had first thought the baby would be born before morning now thought it might not happen until evening. I drove back the fifty miles to our home. The boy was by now lying on his mat, anxiously awaiting word about Mom and the baby. He was disappointed there was no baby as yet, and worried out loud about his mother's condition. I assured him nothing was happening just now and Mom had no pain.

Around eight that evening, after I had been back at the hospital for a few hours, a little girl came into the world. I was in the delivery room and watched the miracle of childbirth for the first time. The load we had borne all during these past nine months was lifted from our shoulders when the doctor said that all indications suggested this baby was normal and in excellent health.

114

Joy was quickly again tempered by grief, however. Despite my gratitude, the agonizing contradiction cut through my soul again that here we had a new child while at home our oldest was so very near death. It made no sense, no sense at all, to have three children for such an unbearably short time.

The boy was overjoyed when I told him he had a little baby sister. He asked about his mother and was relieved that she was doing well. I knelt by his bed and together we gave thanks to God for the miracle of this new sister. He was disappointed that it might be nearly a week before she would come home. I did not tell him that the doctor had decided an extra-long hospital stay would give his mother the rest she could not possibly get at home. There now were three children in our household, each of whom needed almost constant attention.

That night I spent many hours awake again as the boy cried with pain.

eleven ❧

It became obvious that seeing the new baby was the final goal the boy had set for himself in this life.

During that day when I at last went to the hospital to get his mother and new sister, he watched the clock impatiently. When we finally came home he could not see enough of his little sister. We laid her for a while beside him on the mattress. Their heads close together, his blond crew cut, her brown strands, he listened to her breathe as she lay contentedly beside him, her big brother whom she would never get to know. He touched her tiny fingers and counted her toes while our other boy hovered around, for once equally intrigued.

I can see them still, lying on that brown striped mattress, the baby with her tender, fresh skin and beautifully proportioned body and the boy, emaciated and gaunt, his pale, sunken cheeks flushed with the excitement of the moment, his useless legs twisted and motionless, his thin arms protectively around the little girl. His eyes wide-open with the thrill of this marvelous presence of a long-awaited baby sister, hers closed in confident, relaxed sleep. The picture is burned into my memory almost as vividly as that of the shiny basin with the red blob that I had seen three years before. As a symbol of creation at its finest, she represented life and hope for the future. He, death, and the finality with which it intrudes upon God's world and into the life of God's people. Before both of them stretched the great unknown where one can only walk in faith.

"Little girl," I thought in the deep places of my heart, "will you have as much pain as your brother has already experienced? And when the pain comes, what form will it take? Will you be able to bear it? Will the life that we conceived for you be a burden or a blessing? Have we done you a favor? Since you did not ask to come, will you regret at some future date having come? What lies in store for you? God, shelter her in your arms and give your angels charge over her."

From the moment his little sister came home, the boy lost the will to live. If there sprouted in his soul some resentment because she was so healthy and had her whole life before her, while his life was now numbered in mere days, he never indicated. More than likely he felt that life held no more challenges, no more surprises. Perhaps, too, the struggle to stay alive so long, to wait for this momentous day, had been greater than any of us realized, draining him of strength that was no longer replenished.

From a service agency we borrowed a hospital bed that now occupied a corner of the family room. This became his whole world, four walls, a door through which he could no longer move, and one window that gave an occasional glimpse of a world increasingly alien to him. Except for his arms, the boy's body was now completely paralyzed, grotesquely twisted as the muscles contracted through disuse, and finally frozen into one fixed position. He could not even turn over anymore, so it became our chore to turn his wasted body from one side to the other every few hours.

Having lost all sensation and control in the lower part of his body, he now needed diapers. Of all the debilitating things to happen to him, this embarrassment and humiliation grated on him the most. To be like his little sister, dependent on Mom or Dad to change him because he could no longer tell when he needed to go to the bathroom, and to be so twisted that he could not even use the bathroom anymore! Those huge green diapers that we obtained free by the boxful from a local agency were for him the epitome of disgrace and shame. More than ever, he hid in the privacy of his room from all those acquaintances he had known before. Only a few deeply trusted friends were still welcome in his room on those days when his sense of shame was not quite so overwhelming.

Our life began to revolve around that bed as every two hours we cleaned and turned him, a process that went on around the clock. The greatest part fell on my wife during the day. Somehow she blended care for the boy with care for the baby and even managed to do some of the other housework. People began to bring food, so the chore of cooking would be less. Others helped in other ways.

Meanwhile, I carried on as best as possible the duties of the parish. It was a rare week now that I prepared two sermons. We either obtained the services of a relief pastor once each Sunday or else I exchanged pulpits with colleagues in neighboring churches. But other duties could not be transferred to another. The nights were mine, though it soon became obvious I could not possibly be awake seven nights per week. My wife's mother came one or two nights per week; then we found a nurse to help out as well.

Despite our best care and despite the thick sheepskin on which the boy rested, he developed pressure sores on his hips where the bones had lost all their padding. The angry wounds soon deepened until the bones were visible. Now, cleaning and dressing those sores was also part of the bi-hourly ritual. To our relief, the wounds caused no pain whatever because the nerves had already lost their ability to transmit pain.

I barely remember all those tedious chores connected with caring for a dying boy. At the time they seemed so time-consuming and emotionally draining as every few hours we were again confronted with the awful truth that death was already here. Now, they are almost forgotten; it is with effort that I force my mind to disgorge those memories. Perhaps that is because both facts and feelings have been suppressed so forcefully and so deep. As I allow my mind to linger back in that room, I'm conscious again of the pain. While I write this now, years later, tears blur my eyes even though then, when I worked with the boy, I made a concerted effort not to show either surprise or revulsion at his condition.

When caring is something that needs doing, you do it. Complaining does no good; the job *still* needs doing. And so, by the grace of God, you get through each cleaning, dressing, and turning, and prepare for the next time. You ignore the sight and the smells; after a while they become familiar, no longer offensive. You steel yourself against emotions. And you comfort yourself that at least he feels no pain, no physical pain, at any rate. It was, I realize, love in action, that caring that we provided, even though often it seemed more like a duty. But is not this the true nature of love, that one carries out duties especially when they become so intensely revolting and go against the grain?

It was not all a chore, to be sure. I cherish the memories of our talks during those long night hours as the boy grappled ever more persistently with questions of life and particularly questions of dying and the life hereafter. There was the time, when neither of us could sleep, we listened to my favorite oratorio, Felix Mendelssohn's *Elijah*. The boy knew most of Elijah's story; now I called his attention to the emotions of Elijah and the other characters in the story, feelings so poignantly expressed in the masterwork. We listened silently, his hand in mine, as the widow of Zarephat came to Elijah and poured out her anguish when she discovered her only son was dead: "Help me, man of God! my son is sick! and his sickness is so sore that there is no breath left in him! I go mourning all the day long; I lie down and weep at night. See mine affliction. Be thou the orphan's helper! Help my son! there is no breath left in him!" How like her feelings were mine. I whispered to the boy how much it pained me that he was dying and there was no Elijah to heal him.

We listened to Elijah's prayer: "Lord, my God, let the spirit of this child return, that he may again live!" And the boy knew that, though we had both prayed, now there would not be an answer regardless how badly we wanted it.

We listened—I, almost with envy—as the widow poured out her joy after Elijah gave back to her a living son: "The Lord hath heard thy prayer, the soul of my son reviveth! Now by this I know that thou art a man of God, and that His word in thy mouth is the truth. What shall I render to the Lord for all his benefits to me?" And Elijah and the widow answered the question together in a beautiful duet, followed by the chorus: "Thou shalt love the Lord thy God, love him with all thine heart, and with all thy soul, and with all thy might. O blessed are they who fear him! Blessed are the men who fear Him: they ever walk in the presence of peace. Through darkness riseth light to the upright. He is gracious, compassionate: He is righteous."

The boy chuckled as he heard Elijah taunt the priests of Baal time and again because their god did not come to light the altar to prove his existence. He grew thoughtfully silent during Elijah's gentle, unrepeated prayer: "Lord God of Abraham, Isaac and Israel! this day let it be known that

Thou art God; and I am thy servant! O show to all these people that I have done all these things according to Thy word! O hear me Lord, and answer me; and show these people that Thou are Lord God; and let their hearts again be turned!"

"Why did it work for Elijah, Dad, and not for us? Why doesn't God listen to us when we pray? Why do I need to die?"

I had no answer. Yes, what did Elijah have that I lacked? Why does the Bible tantalize us with all those marvelous stories of instantly answered prayer while we continue to grope with silence? It may be true to say, as some people do, that no answer means God has something better in store, but it does not always comfort. If in Bible times people could come with a specific request, and receive it, why can't we do that today and have the same assurance of relief?

I did not share my questions with the boy. Why confuse him further? Instead I said, "I guess God wants you to be the very first person of our family to find out what he looks like, how much he really loves us, and what heaven is like. I wish I could go with you. Heaven sounds so exciting and so beautiful. But God apparently knows that you are now strong enough and old enough to go by yourself."

The choir sang again as we fell silent, each with our private thoughts: "Be not afraid, saith God the Lord. Be not afraid! thy help is near. God, the Lord thy God, saith unto thee, Be not afraid! Though thousands languish and fall beside thee, and tens of thousands around thee perish, yet it shall not come nigh thee."

"But I'm still afraid, Dad—a little, anyway."

As if to take away his final fears, the tenor sang out his words of assurance and consolation: "Then shall the righteous shine forth as the sun in their heavenly Father's realm. Joy on their head shall be for everlasting, and all sorrow and mourning shall flee away for ever."

And the quartet, "O come, everyone that thirsteth, O come to the waters: O come unto Him. O hear, and your souls shall live forever."

Though his eyes, mine too, glistened with tears, the boy whispered softly, "Dad, I think it will be so beautiful there. Do you think I have to wait much longer?"

I shared my conviction that it would not be many more weeks before he would be with God in glory and that he would be able to talk to Elijah himself about all the things we had just heard in the oratorio. But then it was past time to turn him again and our attention quickly descended from heaven to soiled diapers and rotting flesh. Yet how precious were some of those nights where we could talk almost as equals and share in a way that otherwise perhaps would never have happened.

During the day, he still tried to stay busy. While his arms still functioned he glued together tall towers of thin spaghetti. It was a tedious task that occupied a great deal of his time. Each day, though, the towers became less graceful and his frustration greater as his coordination slowly failed. Finally, even this became too much for him. That persistent snake, at work now for so many irresistible months, had almost reached the head. Now there was nothing anymore that the boy could do except lie on one side or the other and watch television or the tantalizing slice of life that showed through the window. The television was perched atop a high cart that we could move to the best viewing position. The window did not move; the world was visible only from his left side.

What is that like, I wonder as I write this, to lie on one side for two hours, unable to move? I decide to experiment, though I know it can never be the same. I, at least, can get up at the end of two hours. More importantly, I

123

can get up any time I want to drink water, go for a walk, take a shower, eat a banana.

I lie on my bed, on my right side. It is a totally different room, in another building and another state. I live all alone in this apartment. After a while I realize I cannot see out of my window because for that I need to lie on my other side. I start to turn, then realize that I may not turn. The thought makes me want to roll over even more. Suddenly it becomes so important to look out the window. Is the sky blue? Are there clouds floating through that little piece of sky at the top of the rectangle formed by the window? If I look carefully, will I be able to see a bird? I want to know, I need to know. But I can't turn. I can only look at the folding doors of my clothes closet. Shadows creep across the room. There must be clouds today!

A fly buzzes somewhere in the room. There are not supposed to be flies here. It is too early for flies. The buzzing continues and I wonder where the fly is. At least I can turn my head a little. That is permitted because the boy could still turn his head. I stretch as far as I can without breaking my self-imposed rules. The fly remains invisible. Then I feel something on my ear, and the buzzing stops momentarily. I shake my head, but an itching feeling continues. Is it the fly? The buzzing starts again, though the itch continues. I want to scratch, but my arms won't bend enough to reach my ear. Another itch starts on my leg. That was something the boy didn't have to worry about since his legs were without feelings. Can I scratch my leg? I decide against it.

From where I lie I can see the clock. Only twenty minutes have passed. It seems like twenty hours. My muscles begin to feel cramped, the compulsion grows to flex them. It dawns on me that a basketball game is about to start on the television. I have forgotten to turn it on, forgotten to move the set into this room. No basketball

124

this afternoon. Perhaps I can watch the final minutes; by then my two hours will be up. Only two hours! Thank God I'm in good health. I only have to lie here two hours.

A car door slams and almost immediately afterward my phone rings. There is a world out there, people who want to reach me. But I am here, confined to this bed for two hours. The phone is in the other room and to see whose car is outside I need to walk to the window. Both are impossible. The world stays out there and I stay here with my thoughts.

An hour. God, only an hour? That is only half-way through this stretch! There's still only the door a few feet from my face. I've memorized almost all features, the shape of the wood grain. Lines swirling around a knot remind me of water in a river swirling around a big rock. On the other panel there seem to be layers of overlapping leaves. Small holes show where someone has once attached a door-length mirror. My body presses against the mattress while my ear begins to hurt. Strange, I've never had these aches when I lie in bed at night. But then I can move around. Now I must lie still. My legs tingle with the effort to keep them in one place.

From the living room my clock chimes the half-hour. My stomach growls because it is now well past my lunch hour. That is another thing I can't do, eat when I want. But the boy was rarely hungry during those last months of his life. I recall how we tried to coax him to eat something, anything. My wife prepared all the things he loved—to no avail. Food held no appeal. The only thing for which he asked without fail was the medicine. His pills punctuated his days. We wondered often whether his pain really was so severe, now that his nervous system no longer seemed to carry messages, or whether he had become addicted to the narcotics. The panic he showed when we tried to delay giving a pill suggested addiction, as did the occasional temporary delirium he showed. But we never made any attempt to end the addiction. It was not important anymore.

Still fifteen minutes till I can get up. By now my body is a mass of tension that throbs through my limbs. I decide to cheat. I get up, feeling a little guilty because the boy could not get up. The best he had to look forward to was two hours on his other side, facing the window.

I look out of the window. The car is gone. I wonder who may have stopped here. Dark grey clouds threaten rain. I don't care. After eating a quick sandwich, I race out the door to go for a walk in the forest.

Behind me lingers the memory of a pale, thin boy lying on a bed for whom walking in a forest was only a vague dream.

twelve ✎

Two or three weeks passed. The highlight of the boy's days came when his little sister spent a few minutes lying in his bed. Sometimes he even held the bottle while she drank with gusto. For the rest, the days and nights were a grinding, monotonous routine of turning him, cleaning and dressing his wounds, and giving him his medication on schedule. The tumors in the boy's lungs did not seriously interfere with his breathing or cause any other discomfort. It was obvious, however, that the illness greedily sapped his strength.

The new bike, barely used and without any sign of wear, stood against the wall of the family room. The boy was still thrilled with it even though he could no longer use it. Gradually, however, it began to represent a problem in the boy's mind. Finally he voiced his dilemma.

"You know, Dad, I wish I'd never gotten that bike. It's causing me nothing but trouble."

"What do you mean? How does it cause you trouble? Do you want me to move it to the basement?"

"No, it's not that. But, you see, I can't use the bike anymore and I can't sell it. How can you sell something that your friends gave you? That wouldn't be right, would it? Besides, then I'd worry about what to do with the money I got for it. If I hadn't gotten the bike, I wouldn't have this problem."

"Well, let's think about it for a few days. What can you do with a bike you don't want to keep and can't sell? Give it some thought."

A few days later the answer came to him, with a bit of help from us. We mentioned that the school for special education where his brother attended used bikes to teach the handicapped children how to ride.

"Do you think they could use my bike?" he said. "How about calling them for me?"

I called the principal, who was delighted with the offer. They would be more than happy to have the bike. In fact, he was willing to drive over, pick up the bike, and thank the boy in person.

The boy wanted no part of that arrangement. "No way, Dad. I don't want that guy to see me like this. Why don't you just bring the bike to them?"

Dutifully, I took the bike to the school. The boy watched with wistful eyes as he saw me wheel it out of the room. Yet another small part of his life was rudely torn off. This gift was a sacrifice, perhaps the greatest he had made thus far in his short life. He treasured that bike so much. Yet it was a willing sacrifice, his own gift deliberately chosen.

A few days later the mailman brought a letter from the principal, thanking the boy for his generosity and assuring him that the bike would be well used and bring happiness to many children in years to come. It was a meaningful gesture on the man's part. Yet, when the school's newsletter arrived some weeks later, I noted with a twinge of regret that among all the donations made to this private facility, the boy's bike was not mentioned. Listed were the large donations from wealthy individuals as well as the generous offerings taken in some area churches. I could not help wonder, as I scanned the list, whether any gift among those so prominently noted represented the givers' greatest treasure, the most precious thing in their possession. How symbolic of our crass commercial approach to charitable giving, I thought, that we recognize the large donations that represent only a small part of the wealth of individuals and corporations. We affix bronze plaques to the doors or windows to remember those "generous" givers, while overlooking the sacrificial mite coming from a widow's poverty or the bike surrendered by a dying boy. But then I remembered our Lord's comments that those honored now have their reward already while secret gifts will be rewarded later when the givers appear in the presence of God.

The boy's predicament with respect to his worldly possessions was not yet resolved, however. The bike was gone, to be sure, but left was the money in his saving account representing the countless cards received from well-wishers over the years. He turned his attention to that next. Right about this time my watch began to show signs of age. Repeated cleanings and adjustments did not solve the problem. It simply was no longer dependable. The boy poured over Sears catalogs and looked at every watch displayed there. Yes, he concluded, he would have enough money for a watch and still have something left over for the other members of the family. He looked at the pages of attractively displayed rings. Finally his decision was made. We were supposed to take all of his money and go shopping with it. A watch for me, with an inscription engraved on the back reminding me where the watch came from, for his mother a ring with three birthstones, one for each child in the family and his in the middle. For his brother and little sister we were also instructed to buy rings. Though his brother was not expected to learn how to read, the boy thought that a ring with a large initial "H" would be meaningful, "H" being the first letter of his brother's first name. For his baby sister he chose a finely crafted ring with a beautiful stone. He had thought of all aspects of the gifts.

"Don't give the kids their rings until they're at least fifteen and will value them. I wouldn't want them to lose the rings."

My wife and I took an afternoon to do his bidding while a kind lady came to stay with the children. Although the boy had given rather specific instructions, we still had some freedom to make our own choices. We went from store to store, comparing quality and checking prices. In the end it appeared there was not quite enough money to do everything the way he wanted it. Rather than disappoint him, we added some of our own and never told him. Why tarnish his final generous moment? We returned home and showed the result of our expedition. The boy was pleased. Now all his problems were solved, with the exception of a closet full of toys that he generously gave to his brother.

It was a bittersweet experience, that shopping trip. We knew that these would be the very last gifts our son would ever give us. He had by now become so weak that we knew his life was numbered in days instead of weeks. Yet he was ready to leave this life. All this activity of dividing his possessions was just a matter of setting his house in order. He had brought nothing into the world and was determined to have nothing left when it came time to leave. He had reached the point where life had nothing more to offer him. He had no more goals left, no more dreams or plans. Lying in that bed in the family room, he became the embodiment of Paul's injunction in Colossians 3:1–4: "Since, then, you have been raised with Christ, set your hearts on things above, where Christ is seated at the right hand of God. Set your mind on things above, not on

130

earthly things. For you died, and your life is now hidden with Christ in God. When Christ, who is your life, appears, then you also will appear with him in glory."

It is strange, now that I reflect on it, that those last days are now a blur. The demanding task of caring for this little boy who was almost totally paralyzed drained every ounce of our strength. There was no time for anything else. I appreciated being in this church where generous allowances were made so I could take whatever time needed to spend on my son's care. My wife and I had little time for each other, too little, in a tragic process that would exact its own price later. The boy's pain began to diminish, though we knew that was no sign of improvement. His need for the narcotics continued unabated; we supplied them without hesitation and with the doctor's blessing.

My struggle over God's will in all this had pretty much subsided. Not that I had found answers or even that I had found ultimate peace. Far from it. I think I will never reach the point where I can consider suffering and death good, even though I can point to good consequences that may flow from those tragedies. It was more that I had reached a point of resignation to the inevitable. There was no longer any question of the boy's surviving. There was no longer any reason to pray for healing or to expect a miracle. All evidence made clear there would be none. Whatever comfort I found in all this was inspired mostly by the boy's process of spiritual growth. He no longer expressed doubt or fear. He no longer wished for healing. Never now did he talk about things he would do when he got better. All his talk was about what heaven would be like and what he would do there. He had become, in every respect, a citizen of heaven even though he never, as best as I can remember, specifically said that he accepted Jesus as his Savior. But it was obvious that he had. In everything, his comfort rested on what Jesus had done for him and was doing for him. He thought of Jesus as a friend and looked forward to meeting him.

It reminds me of the introduction to the Heidelberg Catechism, used by many Prostestant denominations:

Q. What is your only comfort
    in life and in death?

A. That I am not my own
      but belong—
      body and soul,
      in life and in death—
         to my faithful Savior Jesus Christ.
   He has fully paid for my sins with his precious
      blood,
   and has set me free from the tyranny of the devil.
   He also watches over me in such a way
   that not a hair can fall from my head
   without the will of my Father in heaven:
   in fact, all things must work together for my
      salvation.
   Because I belong to Him,
   Christ, by his Holy Spirit,
   assures me of eternal life
   and makes me whole-heartedly willing and ready
   from now on to live for him.[5]

Despite our faith in God's guiding hand, we nevertheless looked forward to the boy's dying. Partly because there was no reason for him to suffer any more than he already had. For him dying would be an undeniable and glorious gain. He would be forever with the Lord. But also partly because we so desperately needed an end to this process of letting go. It seems selfish, I realize, to wish your child's death, to long for the day that you won't have to change one more diaper, clean out those gaping pressure sores, turn him onto his other side. We longed for an end to this whole process that simply went on and on and on.

I have since learned that it is a common feeling. Many people experience it though most are ashamed to own up to it. After all, it seems so monstrously callous to wish someone dead. And yet, it is a normal response, I think, for people who want life to continue and who are weary of existing side by side with death. Much though it may hurt to let a loved one go, the loved one's dying is an increasingly painful reminder of one's own mortality. And who, after all, has the stamina to stare indefinitely into the small, threatening circle of the guns of the firing squad?

Just as the boy had made his arrangements for his coming death, so we began to make ours. We asked a pastor friend who lived a thousand miles away whether we could call on him to conduct the funeral service when the time came, to which he agreed. I visited the funeral director with whom so often I worked at the funerals of others. This time it was personal. This time the arrangements were for my own son, my precious one, whose life could not be ransomed for all the money in the world. We chose a casket and a cemetery plot. We made all other arrangements that could be made, asking friends to be pallbearers, selecting music for the organist—including Schubert's beautiful rendition of the Twenty-third Psalm. In the end, the whole theme of the funeral service revolved around the concept of the Lord being a Good Shepherd whose care is always sufficient. It was a painful task, this planning for a death that had not yet taken place, but it was necessary, almost therapeutic. Reviewing all these details made real beyond doubt that the boy's death was imminent, that God was asking us to let him go. It was practical too. Once he died there would be little enough time to think and plan. So why not do it now?

Thanksgiving came and passed, a quiet, subdued event. Christmas was just a few weeks away. The nursing care for the boy continued according to the now-familiar routine.

We still had our private talks, he and I, in the quiet of those nights when neither could sleep. It seemed we had touched on all subjects and there was really little more to be said. Despite our age difference, we were in many ways equals. In matters of faith, he was my superior. He never doubted anymore, while the best I could come up with was "Lord, I believe, help my unbelief."

The boy watched the television commercials offering their mouth-watering selection of attractive toys that ordinarily would have sent him making a long wish-list. This time he was not swayed by the alluring scenes. When he heard us talk about having to buy some presents he quickly expressed his opinion. "Don't buy me any presents. I don't have pain anymore, and Jesus will soon come to take me to my new home."

A few days later he talked to his mom about baking chocolate-chip cookies, always his favorites even while he rarely ate any now. The boy asked whether it could be done right now. He wanted to help put on the chips. His mom promised the cookies would be baked the next day and, yes, he could help. He was pleased. That night it was my turn to stay with him. Sometime during that night, as I read my Bible, the boy asked me what I was reading. I told him and he asked me to read it to him. It was from Joel 2 where the prophet talks about the coming Day of the Lord:

> And afterward,
>   I will pour out my Spirit on all people.
> Your sons and daughters will prophesy,
>   your old men will dream dreams,
>   your young men will see visions.
> Even on my servants, both men and women,
>   I will pour out my Spirit in those days.
> I will show wonders in the heavens
>   and on the earth,

134

blood and fire and billows of smoke.
The sun will be turned to darkness
    and the moon to blood
    before the coming of the great and
    dreadful day of the Lord.
And everyone who calls
    on the name of the Lord will be saved.

The boy was pensive for a while. Then he said, "I guess I won't see that, will I, Dad?"

I pondered his question, then gave my explanation. "I don't quite know what to say about this. In a way the Holy Spirit is already given to people today. He surely is at work in you, I can tell. Otherwise you would not love Jesus as much or look forward to being with him in heaven. Only the Holy Spirit can give you that longing. And you will see visions. It will only be a little while and you will see God himself, sitting on his throne in heaven. That is the greatest vision of them all. And you'll see it before any of us in this family. But as for the specific day that the Bible calls, 'The Day of the Lord,' no, you won't see that, unless people in heaven are in some way involved in it too. I may not see it either, for that matter. No one knows just when that day comes. It doesn't really matter when it comes, anyway. There is only one thing that matters. That is whether you love Jesus now and believe that he saved you by dying for you on the cross."

"I believe that, Dad."

Dawn came at last and, after my wife awoke, it was my turn to go to bed for some much-needed sleep. Less than a half-hour later, my wife awoke me because the boy seemed different. I quickly dressed and went to his bed. As we bent over him, the boy seemed asleep. With difficulty he opened his eyes and whispered something. To this day I am not sure whether it was, "Hi, Dad," or "Bye, Dad." But having said that, he closed his eyes. Instinctively we knew that the moment of parting had come.

We called our family doctor who rushed over with his nurse. By the time he arrived the boy was loudly gasping for breath. After examining him, the doctor suggested we take the boy to the nearby community hospital where oxygen might make him a bit more comfortable. I questioned his decision because I really wanted the boy to stay right here at home and die in familiar surroundings. Finally I gave in, a decision I still regret.

Just then the doorbell rang. When I answered, there was the boy's kindergarten teacher of three years ago, when all this had started. She was a gentle grandmotherly woman whom the boy had always loved. In her hand she had a wrapped present.

"It is for the boy, and I thought I better give it now, rather than wait until Christmas."

I thanked her and told her that it was too late, that the boy just slipped into a coma and was dying. Tears welled up in her eyes. She grasped my hand and whispered, "And I intended to bring it yesterday. Perhaps your other boy will enjoy it instead."

When we opened the present later we saw a manger scene with all the tiny figures glued down so a sick boy could have it on his bed without losing any pieces. But he never saw it.

I brought my car to the door and, for the last time, carried the boy in my arms to lay him on that bed in the back seat. As we walked through the door, I explained to him what was happening, unsure whether he could still hear me. At the hospital, the young nurse's aide assigned to monitor the oxygen supply for the boy turned out to be a girl from our congregation who in the past had often been his sitter. My wife and I took turns sitting by the bed. My wife's parents had come to be with us, along with two neighboring ministers summoned by someone.

Less than two hours passed. I sat by the bed and held the boy's hand, noticing that it was gradually becoming colder and no pulse was detectable. He lay motionless like he had done from the beginning. His breathing became more shallow and finally was barely noticeable. I kept watching the boy's neck where a vein still showed a faint pulse. Then the pulse beat was gone.

"I think he's dead," I said. "Someone call the doctor."

The doctor needed only a few seconds with his stethoscope to confirm what we already knew.

"I'm sorry, but the poor boy is gone."

I rested my head on the bed beside my dead son's hand and wept without restraint, heart-rending sobs expressing all the grief of the past three years but, until now, almost always suppressed. On my back I felt the consoling touch of a man's hand.

Someone else comforted my wife.

thirteen ❧

When we returned home from the hospital just after noon an air of unreality pervaded the house. It seemed devoid of life and engulfed in an eerie silence. In the family room, the empty hospital bed was a painful reminder of the boy's existence, and the sheets and blankets, thrown back in disarray, gave mute testimony to his sudden departure. Slowly the agonizing truth seeped into our minds that he would never return. We no longer needed the bed or the sheepskin or the box with green diapers. The tape and bandages beside the bed were superfluous, and the boy would never again ask for one of the pills from the now-familiar plastic container. He would never again ask for anything, nor ever need anything. It hardly seemed possible that he was gone. He was still so young. He had lived only nine years, three months, two days. And now his life was over, a big fat period placed where for other little boys and girls life still beckons with all its enticing promises.

He had lived almost thirty-nine months after the initial diagnosis, two-and-a-half years more than the six months predicted by the pathologist with his shiny basin. Some of them, the good months, went all too quickly; others, the months of suffering, dragged by at a snail's pace. In all of them, we lived under a cloud of doom, though at one point the cloud took on a golden lining when we thought the boy would be cured. But despite our prayers and the prayers of literally hundreds of friends and acquaintances, the cure had not come. Thirty-nine months, the same number as the Old Testament books. As a friend suggested later, the boy briefly lived in the period of promises that can only find their fulfillment in Jesus Christ the Messiah. Then he went on to claim those promises and experience their unfolding in a new age, where Christ is—in a timeless age that never ends.

As I stared at the empty bed, the promise of Jesus flashed through my mind, given when the disciples were frustrated because they could not drive out a demon: "Then the disciples came to Jesus in private and asked, 'Why couldn't we drive it out?' He replied, 'Because you have so little faith. I tell you the truth, if you have faith as small as a mustard seed, you can say to this mountain, "Move from here to there" and it will move. Nothing will be impossible for you'" (Matthew 17:19–20).

That our faith was lacking I would readily admit. But was there not one single person among all those praying who had the kind of faith that can move not only mountains but tumors? And if there are no such people, why did Jesus dangle the promise before us like a carrot at the end of a stick that we can never reach, no matter how hard we try, because the stick is tied to our backs? Whatever Jesus meant, for us it has not worked. I felt a sense of failure, of having been weighed and found wanting. Yet at the same time I wondered whether perhaps our prayers had been selfish rather than selfless. Surely the glory now revealed to the boy far outweighed his temporary sufferings and our permanent loss. But though my head said one thing, my heart spoke another language that brought tears to my eyes.

At home, numerous phone calls needed to be made to

notify our far-flung family that the boy had gone to be with the Lord. A few men came to dismantle the bed and remove it, along with all those memories of the little boy who had lived out his last months and finally gone to sleep in that familiar bed. Now it would go somewhere else, to another family, to replay the same painful refrain. What stories this bed could tell!

That afternoon, while my wife went with her mother to purchase a new dress for the funeral, I stretched out on the living room floor and turned up the volume of the stereo. As the words and sounds of my beloved oratorio *Elijah* rolled over me, they drowned out every other noise. I was alone and could weep without embarrassment. The discussion of that other night, when my son was still here to listen to me, blended with the music too. Now he was gone forever, shining with the righteous in their heavenly Father's realm, becoming friends with Elijah and Peter and with my father, the grandfather he had never known.

Later we went to the funeral home. There the boy lay, dressed in the coat and turtleneck sweater he had worn for that picture taken almost three years earlier. He had rarely worn it since. Though he was so much older, the clothes still fit. He lay still, like he had during those last hours in the hospital. But it was not the same anymore. This was not my son, this was some wax statue, a mocking caricature that only faintly resembled the spirited boy who had been my son. We had wondered, earlier, whether we should even have his casket open. Sensitive to the boy's embarrassment about his appearance, we did not think it right to allow everyone to gawk at him now, at this shadow of what had once been a healthy child. But when we saw him, we decided it would be all right for others to see him one last time so they could remember him the way he was but also as he had become.

Someone said, "He looks so nice in that coat." I wanted

to scream, "No, he looks horrible. He's dead!" But I said nothing.

We go to such lengths to disguise the reality of death. There was a time when a body remained at home, resting in a plain wooden coffin on a few sawhorses in a darkened room. Closed drapes and dark crepe bore mute testimony that death had intruded into this home. When people mourned it was in the comfort of their own familiar surroundings. When friends came to call, they saw the deceased in the same room where he or she had been seen alive. Death was more real then and blended with life in a healthy manner.

Now the dead are rarely kept at home. The bodies are treated to a beautification process unlike any they have ever experienced before. Powder and rouge are freely used to cover the blemishes of disease and pallor of death. Sunken cheeks are filled out a bit. The bodies are displayed amid flowers and soft lighting. Music floats softly from concealed speakers. We pretend that the person in the shiny casket is asleep when all along we know well it is a sleep from which there will be no awakening in our lifetime. It is all so artificial, a commercial dishonesty to help us escape the reality that some day we will also fall asleep. We push death away, when actually each death should urge us to be better prepared for our own.

We did not go to the funeral home for the visitations. Our friends would come to the house, we knew, and those strangers whom we barely knew we really didn't care to see just now. Besides, we had no stomach for the banalities so often expressed to those bereaved.

The next few days were terribly difficult. The boy was gone, yet we still felt his presence. Repeatedly we got up to walk into the family room because we thought we heard him call or instinct told us it was time to change his dressings and turn him onto the other side. We'd come into the room, and there would be nothing but empty silence—that and the sudden awareness that it was over.

I spoke with one friend of how difficult it was to let him go. He was so little. What parent in his right mind lets a nine-year-old go all alone on a long journey? But our son had traveled beyond our reach, all alone, to a world where we had never been and from which he would never return. Was there for him, though we did not see it, a flaming chariot to carry him into God's presence? Or had angels stealthily come into that hospital room at the very moment when I saw that the vein in his neck no longer pulsed? Why, when angels come, must they remain invisible?

At the memorial service a few days later, the church was packed. Many people had come, some from far away, to share this day with us. The pastor, that good friend of ours, talked about the boy he had known, about the long months of suffering, about the Good Shepherd who leads us even though our way goes through a dark valley, about the bright and glorious future that awaits those who put their trust in nothing else but Jesus Christ as Savior.

The children of the private school where my son had completed almost three years sat in a block toward the front of the sanctuary. They sang a song, chosen by our son as his very favorite, "What a Friend We Have in Jesus." I listened to some of their words.

> Can we find a friend so faithful
> Who will all our sorrow share?
> Jesus knows our every weakness;
> Take it to the Lord in prayer!

After the service, while Schubert's music softly filled the sanctuary, everyone filed past the open casket for a final glance at this little boy for whom so much living had been packed into such a short time. His school friends, most of whom had not seen him for several months, looked at his body with a mixture of curiosity and bewilderment. For almost all of them it was the first time they had seen the body of one of their own, a friend with whom they had played tag, who had eaten at their table and been part of their class. Now he lay cold and still, and they were impressed with the sudden awareness that death does not come only to old grandparents.

Finally came our turn to see once more this little body in which we had invested so much of our love and our time. I gazed at the short blond hair, the pale face that used to smile so much before that horrible pain came, the eyelids closed over the sparkling blue eyes. Those eyes would never open again. The mouth would never again call our name or cry out in pain. Those hands folded on his chest would never again be nestled in mine. We saw the casket being closed. It was time to go.

While a bitterly cold wind howled across the small cemetery and snow squalls swirled around us, we laid our son's body in its final resting place. Numb, both from the cold and the emotions of this moment, I conducted the brief grave-side rites, a final gesture of caring for the son who had meant so much to us. "We are here to lay to rest the body of our Gerard, although we know that he himself is with the Lord in glory. Gerard knew that the invitation was sincere: 'Let the children come to me, and do not hinder them, for the kingdom of heaven belongs to such as these.' He willingly gave away everything he had here in the assurance that what Jesus gives is so much better.

"We are told in the Scriptures, in Revelation 21: 'Now the dwelling of God is with men, and he will live with them. They will be his people, and God himself will be with them and be their God. He will wipe every tear from their eyes. There will be no more death or mourning or crying or pain, for the old order of things has passed away.

He who was seated on the throne said, "I am making all things new." ' Gerard looked forward to being new again.

"So we commit this body to the soil from which the first human body was taken. It will return to dust. But we believe in the resurrection of the dead. We know that Jesus will return, that the trumpet will sound over all these graves, and that this grave too will one day be opened again. We know that Jesus will raise up this body, without the disease that caused Gerard so much pain, but made perfect to resemble the perfect and glorious body of Jesus Christ.

"We do not keep looking at this grave, therefore, for that reminds us always of parting. We look up to heaven instead from where all our help comes, and from where one day our risen Savior will come so that our joy also may be complete."

Then it was time to leave. With a wind chill far below zero it was unwise to linger any more than necessary. Even the tent provided only minimal relief. How hard it is to leave a graveyard when you must leave behind a coffin containing the body of someone so precious. It is like the final tearing of the tissues of one's heart, an unraveling of all those strands that have been intertwined over so many years. Now suddenly there was nothing more for us to do. The center around which our whole life had revolved for so many months was tucked away in the casket and would soon be lowered into the ground. And we turned out backs on that, and we faced a gaping hole in our lives.

Parents are not supposed to bury their children. The old are not supposed to stand beside the graves of the young. It is unnatural. One is not prepared for it. The death of a child tears apart a family like the uprooting of one plant out of a cluster that have been allowed to grow together in one pot. It cannot be done. All those roots become so intertwined over the years that nothing short of violence

145

can separate them. And it leaves all the plants stunted. Sometimes the remaining plants receive such a shock that they never quite grow normally again. Ever afterward, their growth is warped, though in time the empty place may gradually be filled again.

Yet it happens. Death comes to little children like it comes to the old, in a searing, agonizing pain whose scars will always linger and whose memories can so easily again trigger a throbbing anguish. Jean de La Fontaine has written that "on the wings of time, grief flies away." It is not really so, I think. Time only dulls the ache. But when, for whatever reason, we probe beneath the scars, blood flows just like before.

To be sure, it is different for Christians. While we mourn, our mourning is not like that of people who have no hope. As Paul said, "We believe that Jesus died and rose again and so we believe that God will bring with Jesus those who have fallen asleep in him" (1 Thessalonians 4:14). We also believe that none of these things are allowed to happen without bringing with them some ultimate good. God *does* work in all things for the good of those who love him, who have been called according to his purpose. It may take awhile for the good to become evident. Christians bleed and hurt just like non-Christians, and they need the same healing process. Christians need time to put the fragments of their lives back together, to lay to rest those troublesome questions. It may take months or even years. But God has all the patience in the world.

In the end, God will always be victorious. Satan may rampage through the world and through the souls of people, with God's inscrutable permission, and cause indescribable disaster and anguish. When he is finished, however, and arrogantly boasts to God, "Look what I've done," God will silence him with his majestic, "And now look what I can do." Then Satan will shamefacedly slink into the corners of his hell while God goes about his work of redemption and restoration.

Oh, yes, we mourn. The writing of this book represents a tearing at the scars until the blood flowed again—and the tears—and many times I wished I had left well enough alone. But we have hope—bright hope for tomorrow, when all who trust in Jesus Christ as Savior will move beyond pain and grief forever because we shall be forever with the Lord. And it is not just some pipe dream, some opium to stupify and mislead hurting people. It is real, because Christ is real, because in our past there is a blood-stained cross on which the Prince of Glory died. Because of that bloody, pain-filled past we have hope when all things are made new and death shall be no more, nor grief, nor crying.

In a little cemetery in a small, out-of-the-way town there is a tiny marker. It bears only three lines:

1961–1970
GERARD RICHARD OOSTERVEEN
"At Home With Jesus"

Of the three, the last line is the only one that really matters. Everything else represents the past. The last line sums up a glorious, endless future, an adventure that for my son has only just begun. Even if he remembers his life on earth, I am sure his joy has wiped away any recollection of pain.

Expectation

Son of my pride,
essence of dreams
cherished then shattered,
how still now you lie
like a flower, ugly and wilted
after too early frost.

Son of my pride, the laughter
in your voice I shall hear
never again.
Never again
shall I see you
or touch you.
Never again in this life.

So far you have gone,
alone yet not alone.
But time which bears
you away also brings you
irresistibly closer to me.
Though you will come back
to me never again,
I shall go where you are,
son of my pride.[6]

Resurrection

There's a stirring in the earth,
irresistible;
and in the air the sound
of angel wings hovering
over this half-acre of death.
Creative power of God
grasping, lifting, drawing,
reviving. Heaven breaking
the stranglehold of hell
forever.

There's a stirring in the earth;
seed sown in tears
now bursting forth,
with joyous strength reaching,
rising, responding
to light and life
irresistible.
Tomb transformed to womb,
dark cavern of hopeless death
into threshold of vitality
that never shall have end
forever.

Christ is risen,
first-fruits of God's harvest.[7]

notes ❧

1. C. S. Lewis, *A Grief Observed* (New York: Seabury Press, n.d.), 9–10.

2. Helmut Thielicke, *Between God and Satan* (Grand Rapids: Eerdmans, 1958), 6–7.

3. Paul Tournier, *Guilt and Grace* (New York: Harper & Row, 1962), 72.

4. From "Baptism of Infants, Form Number 1," Christian Reformed Church in North America. This form, in its essentials, goes back to 16th Century Reformed Churches in The Netherlands and beyond that to the reformer John Calvin.

5. Question and Answer 1 from *The Heidelberg Catechism*, originally written in 1563 in Heidelberg, Germany, by Zacharias Ursinus and Caspar Olevianus. The quotation is from a translation adopted for official use by the Christian Reformed Church in 1975.

6. "Expectation," previously published in *The Banner*, January 11, 1980.

7. "Resurrection," previously published in *The Church Herald*, April 17, 1981, in *Decision Magazine*, April 1982, and in the *John Milton Magazine*, April 1983.

Too Early Frost
was typeset by
the Photocomposition Department
of Zondervan Publishing House,
Grand Rapids, Michigan
Compositor: Nancy Wilson
Equipment: Mergenthaler Linotron 202/N
Typeface: Goudy Old Style
Editor and designer: Bob Hudson
Printer: Color House Graphics
Grand Rapids, Michigan